I STILL BELIEVE

A MEMOIR OF CHILD LOSS, GUN VIOLENCE, AND NEW PURPOSE

Tiffani Evans

Mullen Press

www.mullenpress.com

Morgan B. Holland /Mullen Press Publishing
808 Gleneagles Ct #42301
Towson, MD 21284
www.mullenpress.com
contact.us@mullenpress.com

I Still Believe/ Tiffani Evans. -- 1st ed.
Paperback ISBN 978-1-954016-13-2
Ebook ISBN 978-1-954016-14-9

My New Purpose

In 2024, my purpose will continue as I help my community. I'm grateful for the new normalcy of life. This definitely wasn't the plan I saw for me, but God is giving me all the tools to not only help myself through this pain, but also help others. In the late summer of 2023, the mothers of S.A.M. (Strong Azz Mothers) had a play, and the outcome was a great success, "Turning Pain into a Purpose: Say My Son's Name." I just want to show my deep appreciation for all the support from my community and all the continuous love I've received from everyone. I am grateful for my family, friends, my church family (Community of Hope AME), Bill Lee Photography, M.A.D. (Making a Difference), Hope in Action, the media, the Peace Academy of DC, Anacostia Park of Friends, Prince George's County Police, County Executive Angela Alsobrooks, State Attorney Aisha Braveboy, and anyone else who has supported this journey.

There is so much more in store for the community and I want to keep helping more parents. I want to keep helping youth sports and provide them with the mental help needed. I want to help continuously change the narrative in my area; the DMV needs me!

Contents

I STILL BELIEVE

Introduction

While I desire for this book to ignite radical, unconscious action in your life that catapults you into a healthier version of yourself, God knows I would have preferred not to have learned to become a better version of myself at the expense of losing my son. Peyton "PJ" Evans was an eight-year-old math whiz and a football phenom. My baby loved football and was amazing at it. He would get up after each play, anticipating the next one. I deeply appreciated my son for choosing me to be his mother, and I had an even greater appreciation for our bond. While he was living,

I took little time to reflect on our lives. Between football practice and tutoring sessions, we were always on the go.

After he was murdered, I lived in a constant state of reflection, only visiting the present. It was tempting to stay in the past because the life I had with my son was just so sweet. I had no regrets about how I raised him, nor any doubts that he would have grown up to be an amazing man. There were times throughout my healing journey when I only had my reflections to comfort me. It was through those reflections—through me stepping out of my body and observing myself, raising my son in my memories—that helped me through the tough moments.

Observing myself teaching him and guiding him through life would lead to me getting emotional each time he demonstrated he heard me and that my words were connecting. What I didn't know was that these memories were teaching me through what I was teaching my son. PJ lived life like he played football, strategically. He listened as I gave him instructions on how to grow and move closer to becoming a responsible man, similar to how he listened to his coach following the play to move the team closer to the goal. It was in this space of reflection that I remembered the lessons I taught my son through my memories of our time together, which jump-started my healing journey.

I realized everyone isn't like me. Some people may have regretted some of their experiences with deceased love ones. Regrettable actions have the power to compound guilt or shame. However, healing is possible for anyone. If you decide to prioritize your healing, you are guaranteed to discover a healthier version of yourself. After my son's murder, people questioned whether I would make it. They wondered how I could make it because they knew how close my son and I were and still are. Many had authentic concern for my mental and emotional health, but I say proudly that, I still believe. I still believe that I will continue to have a glorious life and that life can get better after tragedy. I still believe even more in the majesty of God and lean even heavier on His guidance and understanding. I have always been a believer, and I still am one.

As I tell you the story of the last days of my son's life leading up to the time of me writing this book, you will find various suggestions and techniques to help you on your healing journey. Take notes as you read. Highlight areas that are triggering or suggestions you may find helpful. Perhaps there's something in this book that you can add to your personal tool chest that you can use now or in the future. This memoir is about the loss of my son to gun violence, my journey to healing through the trauma, and finding my purpose through self-discovery. So, grab a pen, notebook, highlighter, and some tissue as we laugh, cry, and heal through the reading of my memoir, I Still Believe.

CHAPTER ONE

My Dream Made Real

Like many parents, thinking about life before our children can seem like a distant reality. Once you have a child, everything about life seems to change in an instant. Unlike many parents, I planned for my PJ. My son was always a part of my life plan and I'm forever grateful that I got to experience the few years we had together. PJ was literally my dream made real.

Graduating college in 2010 was the first time I felt like an actual adult. I mean, I know technically I've been an adult since 18, but after graduating, I quickly knew that I had some decisions to make. Fortunately, I got a good government job, making around $60k-$65k right after college. That was a tremendous deal where I'm from. Growing up in Prince George's County, it seemed that nearly everyone's parents worked for the government in some capacity. As a child, adults use to always encourage us to grow up and to get a good government job. So, I did. Check one off my list of things to do leading up to my ultimate dream: becoming a mom.

With this newfound freedom and stable job, I said to myself, *Why rush this mom thing?* I decided to enjoy life. I caught up with old neighborhood friends, dated around and just had a great time. My plan was always to go to school, get a job, find a wife and have a child. That plan never changed. I was just making sure that I enjoyed myself along the way and didn't see a need to rush anything. Then there was this woman at a party.

My Future Wife

I was always going to gatherings and this one was no different. It was a birthday party for my friend's daughter, so I took my godson, who wasn't even one yet and we went to the celebration. I met a beautiful woman there, and we hit it off right away. I was a free spirit at that time, living my life and talking to multiple women. I wasn't in a rush to settle down. I was more open to the opportunity than to forcing one. Sometime after the party, we connected through a mutual friend, and the rest is history. We talked nearly every day, and it was beautiful. She had an amazing seven-year-old son who was so well-mannered.

After six months of dating, I asked him, "Can I be your mother's girlfriend?"

He replied, "Yes, I think you're nice. I think you treat my mom well."

With her son's approval, I asked his mom to be my girlfriend, and she agreed. We moved in together and started planning a life as a family. It was beautiful. I was always upfront about wanting to carry and birth a child. That was always a part of my plan. So, we discussed it together and figured out how to make it happen. She knew how important it was for me to have a child by a certain age and how badly I wanted to be a mother of my own. So, for the next year, we planned out the entire "getting pregnant" process. As a same-sex couple, there are some extra steps between wanting a baby and conception. However, we figured it out together. We had a long discussion about how we wanted our sons to be biological brothers. So, our seven-year-old's father graciously donated his sperm to make it happen and I am forever grateful.

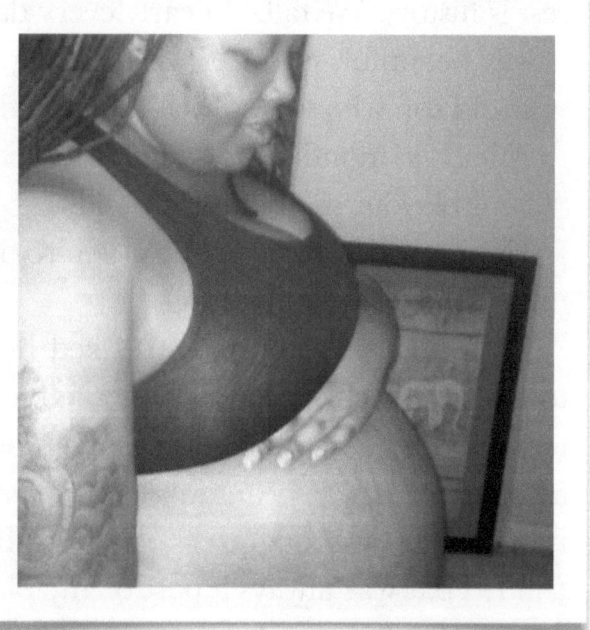

I proposed to my girlfriend around her birthday, and at the time, I was already pregnant with PJ. Life was amazing. We were planning a life together and things were going well. I earned my degree, had a great career, had a beautiful family and was finally pregnant. Things were going as they were supposed to go. Everything was going according to plan.

I gave birth to Peyton John Evans on February 14, 2013, at 26. I'm a preparer. I read some books and watched some videos to get an understanding of the birthing experience. All of that went out the window once those contractions started getting closer and closer. I'm also an overachiever, so I was pushing hard to get my baby out. I knew I had one job that day: deliver that baby.

The doctor said, "Stop pushing. You're about to split yourself."

That scared me a little because I couldn't feel it. I had an epidural, so I couldn't feel anything down there. It just felt like I had to pass a bowel movement and I needed it to come out ASAP. Lo and behold, I ended up splitting myself and my son flew out.

The doctor caught him and joked, "He flew out like a football."

I knew right there that my son was going to be a football star. The doctor unclogged his nose, but PJ didn't cry. He was breathing just fine, but he didn't cry. I was handed PJ with his placenta still attached, and I remember thinking to myself, *He looks smack like my father*. He had a round head and a head full of hair. Mind you, throughout my whole pregnancy, I had crazy heartburn; I was popping Tums like bubble gum. But, oh my goodness, he was so handsome. I could have just looked at him all day. After a couple of minutes, I was knocked out of my trance as they reached to take PJ away to get cleaned up and checked out.

Luckily for me, they did everything in the room, so he didn't have to leave my sight. They took him to the right side of the room and cleaned him up. My mother and at the time my wife were right by his side. They cut the umbilical cord and that's when PJ started crying. They brought him back to me and I just held him in awe. He was all wrapped up tight and I couldn't do anything but stare at him. I was officially a mother. I had a whole child.

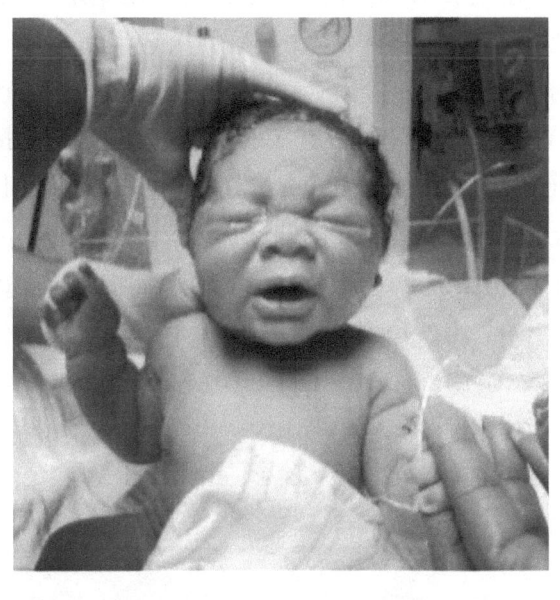

I was crying uncontrollably—happy tears, of course— I was just so happy. My wife at the time, was right there by my side, and I had a fairly large room, so other people could visit me at the same time. My mother was there, my brother (PJ's uncle/godfather), and my wife's sister (who was also PJ's godmother); it was beautiful. I truly felt loved and supported in that moment. PJ stayed in the room for a little while longer with us until he was taken out briefly so he could take all of his tests. Then he came right back to me. I gave birth at Holy Cross Hospital in Silver Spring, Maryland. At that time, it wasn't standard practice to keep babies in a nursery. Your baby stayed with you the whole time. Even though he was only a couple of hours old, I felt like a part of me was missing when the nurses took him for that brief period. I loved the fact that PJ stayed with me and I loved the room I was in. The room was humongous. Everybody who was important to us was there. It was a beautiful moment.

PJ AND HIS BIG BROTHER

Before my son, I was such a stickler for time. I had a plan for everything. I thought I could control my life if I planned it out in detail. Do this in three months, have this in one year, and be this by this age. I was rigid about that before PJ. Now that my son is deceased, I enjoy the moments more. I'm not obsessed with trying to control time. I'm more interested in enjoying time and enjoying life. My son taught me the importance of that. After PJ was born, I was kind of proud of what I'd accomplished so far in life. I had my degree, a great job, a wife, and a family. I felt my life was going according to plan. Then, without my permission, the plans changed.

Adjusting to Single Parenthood

At 26, I was married with two sons. I claimed my wife's son from a previous relationship as mine. He's still my son to this day. Married life with two children had its difficulties. One day, my wife and I decided the downs outweighed the ups, and we got a divorce. At the time, my eldest son was 12, and my youngest, PJ, was three. Our sons had a good, comfortable life and then their lives changed forever. PJ had a difficult time during our separation because us being a family of four and living together was all he ever knew. He didn't understand why we were moving and why he couldn't see his brother and mom every day. He asked questions I couldn't answer in a way that satisfied him, so he started to whine and cry often.

I did not know what to do initially. I was the provider. I took care of the bills and made sure everyone had what they needed. My ex-wife was the nurturer. She handled the whining and emotions of our children way better than me. So, while PJ had to make some adjustments, so did I. I had to learn how to be not only the provider, but also the nurturer. I had to be everything that PJ needed me to be and I was committed to becoming the mom that PJ more than deserved.

I hugged and loved PJ, but not like my ex-wife used to. I was the more dominant parent, the more masculine parent. All I knew was working. I'm talking about how, as soon as I left my full-time job, I would go to Uber for about four hours to make $500. I was accustomed to getting home at around 7 at night on Fridays and Saturdays; I worked as a bouncer at a club. I mean, I was always working. All I knew was to work and provide. I would work long hours and bring all the money straight home to my wife. That was my role. I played my position. That's what I knew how to do. I was the parent who provided.

My ex-wife bought the kids' clothes; hell, she bought my clothes. She made sure there were groceries in the house. She was the house manager. I didn't have to do any of that stuff. Now, I have to buy my son's clothes. I can wash clothes and put them on him, but I called my ex-wife about things that I probably should have known since I, too, was PJ's parent. I had to learn for myself how to do all the things my ex-wife used to do for us.

When my ex-wife started dating, what I felt was super-fast, really messed my head up and snapped me into a new reality: I am a divorced, single mother, and I have to figure this out. I cried for almost a week. It was December and Christmas was coming up. I had to pick out all of PJ's presents alone. My ex-wife came over on Christmas and it was awkward because she was already in a new relationship. And then, I found out that she was pregnant. Everyone feels differently about this, but I was surprised by the thought of her messing around with men again so soon after our almost 5-year relationship ended.

At that moment in time, I didn't know for certain what God had in store for me, but I learned I had to figure it all out fast. PJ was three at the time and we both ended up having some time on our hands. I couldn't have my baby sitting around bored. I wanted him to do an activity or play a sport. It didn't really matter what activity or sport he was doing, as long as he was happy.

We tried flag football early in the new year, right before he turned 4 in February. It was a hit. He loved it and that was it. I felt like I understood what my new assignment was. Football was fun for PJ and a catalyst for me to truly discover and cultivate my nurturing skills. I was determined to be all my son needed me to be and I was prepared to make all the necessary sacrifices to do so.

My ex-wife was, at the time, dealing with a lot of guilt in my opinion. She was battling with the emotions and feelings that she hadn't processed from our separation in 2016. The last time she saw PJ was about two months after his birthday in February 2017, when he turned four. After a lot of back and forth, she stopped seeing PJ for a minute. I know my ex-wife lives with the guilt of not being there like she should have, but I reassured her that we both made mistakes with our son.

This is why I feel like when people are in same-sex relationships and they decide to have a child, have your own. Moving so fast in our relationship and not handling the discussions that we needed to have about the children, my ex-wife felt like she could move on from the both of us without consequence. If I learned anything throughout the separation, it's to have uncomfortable conversations sooner rather than later, especially when it's about children. Things got bad at times and I took it upon myself to cut ties with everything because I was being selfish and immature. As time went on, I put my emotions aside because my sons were getting the short end of the stick.

However, when my ex-wife started dating her new husband, I became extremely concerned about who would be around my kids.

Our oldest was 12, and while he was her son, biologically, after we got married, he became our son. Unfortunately, after we divorced, he stayed with my ex-wife, so seeing him was cut short a lot of the time. One day, while being a curious 12-year-old, my eldest son went into his mother's room and found a gun that belonged to her then-boyfriend. My son shot the gun, and the bullet ricocheted off the wall, nearly hitting him. I can't lie; my ex-wife never told me that this happened because she knew I would flip! I only found out when my 12-year-old son told me nervously and begged me not to tell his mom that he had told me. That was a secret that I couldn't keep as a parent. At that time, a three-year-old PJ would be going to her house while I worked part-time jobs in the evening. At this point of frustration, I couldn't have my youngest son go to her house, where things like this were happening, and she was trying to keep it from me.

I confronted my ex-wife and said, "We need to have a sit-down."

"For what?" she replied slightly annoyed.

"Well, my son just told me he shot off your boyfriend's gun, and the bullet ricocheted off the wall and could have hit him," I said sternly.

She replied quickly, "I've handled the situation."

"We still need to talk," I insisted.

"Well, nobody is talking about the girls you have around PJ," she snapped.

"Do you want to meet her?" I asked. "Because you can meet her, but I need to meet the dude that's got this gun around my 12-year-old son. We all have times when we are irresponsible, but this is unacceptable. At least get a gun safe or put it somewhere where a child can't find it."

My ex-wife huffed as she said, "Well, you're not going to meet him. I don't understand what's the point of you meeting him because, like I said, I've already handled the situation."

"Oh, okay. Well, until I meet this nigga, Peyton John Evans will not be coming over to your house."

And that's where that shit stopped. I believe that she still deals with a lot of guilt from that situation because I believe that she felt that I tried to control her with PJ, and I'm just like, no... At the end of the day, it's safety first. If I could control her biological son, I would not allow him to be around that fool either. Now, my oldest son is 20, and his mother has a difficult time controlling him. He's grieving and figuring out life right now, and it's hard for him. Sometimes, he has unhealthy, toxic coping mechanisms. I can imagine that as a child, he felt like he had to choose even when he confided in me about firing the gun. That wasn't his place. He shouldn't have had to tell me that; his mother should have told me. He should have been protected more as a child, and sometimes I think that now, as an adult, he is paying for that lack of safety that he didn't have as a child.

I hurt till this day when my oldest son hurts. Yes, I took PJ from that situation, but I question whether I fought hard enough for my oldest son. When I took PJ away for his safety, and my ex-wife didn't fight for him, I didn't fight for my oldest son. I should have negotiated better and fought hard for his safety, too. A part of me wonders if I let him down. My oldest son was created with my ex-wife and her ex-husband. I didn't have the authority to speak over him like I had the right to speak for PJ.

PJ AND HIS BIG BROTHER

I frankly don't know if I had the capacity to fight for my oldest son. I was losing it. After the divorce, I had to figure out how to be a nurturer on top of a provider while battling depression. It was hard with a lot going on. I was just so thankful to have my mother because she stepped up and just took PJ over for me. She knew I was just going through the motions of trying to figure out what to do, how to move, how to maneuver. I got a kid that I have to raise by myself. That was a lot for me to try to understand and process. And so my mom helped me out a lot. And after a while, I started talking and dealing with somebody. So, I was doing the absolute most at one time.

I ended up finding out that the lady I was dealing with was pregnant while we were dating. That added another layer of complication. I didn't need to go through any more surprises. I was already going through figuring out how to be a single mom and I'm still grieving my divorce. It was just so much going on in my life. I still sacrificed and made things happen. I stayed with my mother for three years. After that, I felt like it was time for PJ and I to leave. My son was going to first grade and I felt like I needed stability for PJ. So I wanted to move. It was time for me to live on my own. I had never had my own place before, where I paid the bills by myself and I wanted to know how that felt.

I was dead serious. I started looking for a house in May and I moved in September just like that. I showed my son what true sacrifice looked like. Instead of eating out, we saved money and ate in the house. We got on track to get our house and we stacked our bread. I started putting furniture on layaway and paying for it. I just wanted the best for my son and I was determined to get it for him, no matter the cost.

When it was time, I took my son with me to closing on September 4, 2020. I'll never forget it. I explained that this is what sacrifice looks like. He smiled as I happily signed a million papers. It was just a blessing for him to experience all of that with me and see where we went from damn near not having anything, living with my mom, to owning a house. Even though we were living with my mom, I felt like we were homeless. I so desperately wanted to give my son a home of his own and I did. And this is what the pickup looks like when you sacrifice. So, overall, if I had to define motherhood for me, it would be sacrifice.

PJ WORKING OUT

Motherhood Was Defined by Sacrifice

As I learned to be and do all the things PJ needed, I learned first-hand how motherhood was defined by sacrifice. I have sacrificed not only my body, but my time, my finances, my mental capacity and so much more. Motherhood requires sacrifice and I wouldn't change any of it for the world. Even when times are dark and there's only $20 in your account until you get paid next Friday, it's all worth it. All of the sacrifices helped me to better appreciate my son ten times over because he got to experience unconditional love from me, his mother. That mother's love that would give you her last fry on her plate. The love that would starve so their child could eat. No one will ever love you like your mother.

Now, we aren't talking about those messed-up mothers. We are talking about sacrificial mothers. Those "by any means necessary" mothers. Look, man, I embraced mother-hood. I love motherhood. I adored the sacrifices. If I could change anything in the world, it would be nothing, because I know for a fact that I gave that boy the best of me. I loved all the struggles. I loved my son unconditionally, and I know I did my best, so much so that there wasn't much more I could do.

That's why, when I talk to mothers who lost their children, I feel like some of them live with some type of guilt. I also think that guilt is why they can't heal properly because they didn't sacrifice the way they should have with their children. I believe that when you do your absolute best and things still don't work out as you planned, you don't have heavy guilt. I can sit comfortably with the decisions I made as a mother and say with my whole chest that I did my absolute best. I don't live with any guilt regarding how I raised my son. My son, my PJ, knew for a fact that Mommy did it all. He saw Mommy making things work.

CHASE YOUNG OBSERVING PJ

Before PJ passed away, he had lineman training that was $250 a week. Then, he had another trainer that was $200 a month. I'm like, "Oh Lord, that's nearly $500 down right there." I had just bought a house. I had a mortgage, house bills, and more bills that could've been paid with that money, but I made the necessary sacrifices to make sure my son had what he needed. I do my best not to judge other parents, but sometimes I find it so disappointing when parents don't give their children the best they have. I understand not being able to give a lot, especially if you don't have it. However, with a little sacrifice, some parents can do more than what they are doing for their children. Sometimes, I didn't even interpret my sacrifices as sacrifices because I wanted to do whatever it took to make sure PJ had the best life. I just knew it was labeled a sacrifice because a transaction occurred. Perhaps I spent some money or lost some sleep, but either way, it was all worth it. In fact, I welcomed it. The investment in my son and his future was worth it and I'd do it again in a heartbeat.

CHAPTER TWO

Creating His Own Mark

We're going to start off when my baby was a newborn, alright? As a newborn, my little man had personality, even while I was pregnant. It's crazy because when I was pregnant with PJ, he was such a calm baby inside. He would kick throughout the day, and then at night, he slept. So, when I had him, I'm like, man, I'm about to be up all night. I ain't going to be getting any sleep.

Then, when he was born, he barely cried. So, I knew he wasn't going to be a crybaby.

As an infant, PJ was not normal. He slept through the night. I would wake up to check on him and he'd still be asleep. If he did wake up, I just breastfed him, and he went right back to sleep. I got great rest when PJ was an infant. I wasn't sleep deprived at all.

He was an awesome baby. Always quiet, always smiling. He had a dimple just like me; I have one dimple and he had the same thing. And he was always a happy baby, just smiling. Quiet, cool, and collected. Everybody wanted to watch him, and it was so crazy because I was so hesitant about letting people watch him, but I knew he was a good baby. I had actually gone to Hawaii when PJ was three weeks old. I went to Hawaii on a trip that was paid for, and my mother was singing his praises to me when I returned, talking about how he was such a good baby.

As a toddler, PJ loved to dance. He was a dancer. When he heard a beat, he just started bouncing to the beat. He danced to commercials. Man, he would dance to all types of music and he learned dances as a toddler. I'm talking about as soon as he started walking. I got videos of him just dancing, just beating it.

Like, in rhythm and everything. He was a happy baby and he was just as happy as a toddler.

PJ'S FIRST BIRTHDAY

As he got a little older, you know, toddler-hood stopped at around four years old. He was still the same way. He was kind of shy at first, but after his first day of school, he was just a chill kid. He was such a good baby that he made me feel like I could do this a couple of times. He had my personality. He was such a cool kid. He was just happy. He was loving. Everybody loved PJ because he was just friendly. He was a lovable kid. He wasn't too grown up. He knew his place, and he was just a great kid, a great toddler and a great baby. He potty trained early. I think I potty-trained PJ at three years old. He was just easygoing and smooth-sailing.

THREE YEAR OLD PJ

The one thing PJ did that annoyed me was that he would wait until I got somewhere and then tell me he had to go to the bathroom. That was the only thing that drove me crazy. I'm thinking to myself, *We were just in the house. Why don't you poop in the house?* We would go out to the mall and then PJ had to poop. Go to Target; he had to poop. At the football game, he had to poop. It seemed that the boy's bowels hadn't started moving until we left the house.

He was shy in school for a moment but always well-behaved. One of his teachers, Ms. Brooks, whom I still see sometimes, came to his funeral. She spoke so highly of my son. He was her favorite kid. You know how teachers always try not to say that, but she did.

She'd be like, "That's my favorite kid."

If the teacher asked PJ to do something, he was going to do it. He didn't talk back. He always did what he was supposed to do, like be respectful to adults and all that. He was that kid—a great kid. He was always willing to help anyone in the class if they didn't understand something. He loved to help people. He had close friends. In pre-K, there was this little girl that he had a crush on. He fell hard, talking about her all the time, and I mean all the time. She was a cute and smart little girl. Once he started elementary school, he was the same way. He always liked the cute, smart, quiet, chill girl in class.

PJ AND HIS GIRL BEST FRIEND

He didn't like the wild, loud girls, no matter how cute they were. I guess the smart part was non-negotiable for him, but so was being cute. I couldn't be mad at him. It made me proud to know that even as a child, he had an attraction to the type of partner that I'd imagined him with as an adult. Cute, smart, and chill. I was happy for my son and his future.

PJ and His Great-Grandmother

PJ was the baby in the family at the time. He was the great-grandson of my grandmother, who was 90. Well, she was 90 when I had him and they were born on the same day. PJ was her baby for real for real. He was her baby until she closed her eyes and transitioned to the other side. My son would lie in bed with her when she was in hospice care. They were extremely close. She was his great-grandmother and they had a bond that no one could break.

When my grandmother did pass, that crushed him. My grandmother would call him every morning before school and speak life into him before he started his day. So when she passed, it was extremely hard on him when he no longer got his morning calls. The silence almost served as a reminder that she was gone. She had passed in July, and PJ went to school in August, so it was an adjustment for him. I got him a chain with a picture of him and my grandmother together in her hospice bed when she was holding him. I took the picture and gave him the chain for Christmas that year.

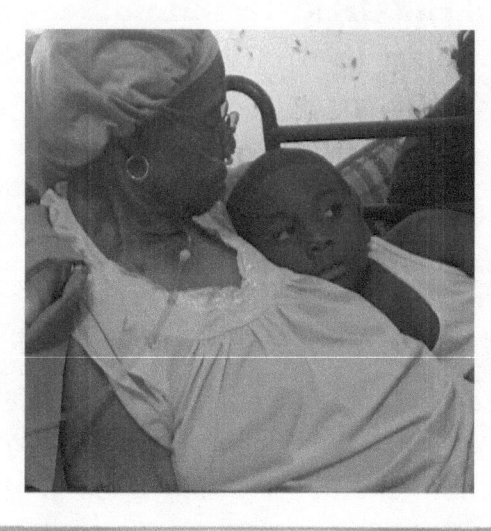

PJ AND HIS GREAT-GRANDMOTHER

I did the best I could to help my baby process the death of his great-grandmother. I understood that was a major loss in his life, and I couldn't just ignore his feelings. Children have feelings surrounding death, too. I didn't bury the chain with him, though. I kept it because now I have both of my angels on it. So, I wear it all the time.

I'm glad that I had PJ in a private Christian school at the time because he knew about God, scriptures, and angels. I still have videos of him reciting scriptures off the top of his head. He had a little understanding of how life worked. He knew about Heaven and Hell. He knew God; my son had a relationship with God.

PJ WITH HIS FAMILY

So that helped me a lot with helping my son deal with the death of his great-grandmother. Trauma is hard, but getting children and some adults to understand the effects when the transitions happen is the hard part. Some people just move on, go on to business as usual, and try to act like they are over it, suppressing their emotions. That's extremely unhealthy, and I didn't want that for my son. I was more emotionally mature than my son and I was having a difficult time with the loss of my grandmother, so I knew my son was having a hard time, too. I made it my business to provide a safe space for him to process his emotions.

I told his teacher about the loss of his great-grandmother so she could let me know about any changes in his behavior. He had just lost a precious person to him and he had never experienced death before. He didn't get a chance to meet my dad because he transitioned when I was seven months pregnant. PJ knew that my dad had passed, but he never met him, so he didn't know what it felt like to lose someone he loved. He didn't know what that looked like until his great-grandmother.

He did well, though. I tried to talk to him every morning to give him some of that consistency that he had with his great-grandmother's morning talks. I prayed with him and helped him to understand that he could still talk to my grandmother through prayer. My son told me that his great-grandmother was his favorite lady. And I loved that because, at the end of the day, every mother wants to be their child's favorite person, right? But my grandmother was that person for him. He could never get in trouble in her eyes; you couldn't fuss at PJ in front of her. She was very loving and protective of him and him of her.

Introduction to Football

Going through my divorce was difficult. PJ and I had a lot of time on our hands, and we had to get out of the house. We had to do something because PJ was three at the time and had a lot of energy that he needed to burn off. I kept seeing my friends posting football stuff on social media and I thought to myself, *Can PJ play? I wonder if they have football for three-year-olds?* I reached out to one of my friends, and they gave me some information on a team my son could play on, and PJ took off from there. My son fell in love with football the first day he played. He was doing drills and everything at age three with middle school kids; he would mimic whatever the older kids did. So, he would just follow the big kids in front of him as they did the drills. He would do the drills successfully. He would mess up sometimes because he had shorter legs, but he would keep doing it until he got it right. He loved football and was in heaven.

PJ PLAYING FOOTBALL

When his first practice was over, I asked three-year-old PJ, "Do you like football? Do you want to stick with this?"

He eagerly replied, "Yeah! I like this! This is fun!"

He's been a football player from that moment until he died. He literally played football an hour before he died. I introduced him to other sports, like basketball, around the age of six, and he was playing with eight-year-olds, but it wasn't his main focus. He enjoyed it, but not as much as he enjoyed football.

PJ played both offense and defense. Sometimes, it felt like my baby was on the field the entire game. He was a defensive end on defense, and on offense, he was a guard, which is a lineman, on the offensive line. So, he blocked for the quarterback and running back. His two main positions were a defensive tackle and an offensive guard. It was a great way for my son to burn off some energy and he didn't complain about it. He enjoyed the game. He was so mild-mannered, so it was probably nice to blow off some steam for fun. He often played the whole game, never getting a break, but he enjoyed it. He was a big boy for his age and the team needed him. The other boys on the team played well with PJ and all pulled their weight.

Football also gave PJ an opportunity to talk trash on the field. He was six years old and talking big trash. It was a part of the game, so everyone did, especially after a tackle or something. His trash-talking skills got better the older he got. Thank goodness. You know, sometimes kids say things that don't make the most sense at the moment, but PJ got better and better at everything he did. And the better he got, the higher his confidence got.

I always told PJ, "Stay humble, but talk your truth slim."

When PJ was taken from me, he was already known as a football phenom at age 8. In addition to being great at football, he was great at so many other things. People would continuously tell me how bright my son's future was. PJ was so well-mannered I never had to talk to him too much about his behavior and he was never disrespectful. If I asked him to do one thing, it took that one time for me to say it. You know, some kids, you just gotta keep repeating yourself. Yeah, that wasn't a problem for me. We would go out, and people would make comments like, "I'll take your kid any day." And I don't just say these things because it's my kid or because PJ is deceased; I say it because it's true.

How PJ Handled Obstacles

While PJ was excelling on the field, he also had to maintain great grades. When he was in first grade he ended up falling behind in his reading. He was always an expert at math, never having an issue with it. He had the highest scores in math in first grade, so he was considered a math wiz for first grade. However, he struggled with reading because of his low confidence when it came to reading aloud. So, I went to his class one day, and I talked to his teacher.

"What do we have to do to get him to come up in reading? You and I must come up with a plan to help my son to improve his reading skills. I'm the adult, his parent, so I'm going to do my homework at home so he can be better."

She gave me my homework to do.

"Make him read a book every day out loud," his teacher replied. "If he stumbles over a word, make him pause, take a breath, then try again."

When the pandemic happened, PJ was above reading because I stayed consistent with what his teacher asked me to do as a parent and his teacher was doing her part at school. He read the objective in front of the class out loud one day when I was sitting in his classroom. He did so well. He read big words and everything in front of his class and that was a huge deal because, at first, he lacked the confidence to read in front of people. He eventually got comfortable with reading aloud. I consistently built him up at home, encouraging him to let him know it's okay to make a mistake, you just take a breath, you know, and read it over again. His confidence level started building back up, just like in football.

I wanted him to have the same confidence in reading that he had in math and football. As the pandemic ended, he was above reading level. The math came easy to him. In pre-k4, he was good with numbers. I don't know what it was, but he could really add and subtract in his head at a young age. In kindergarten, he could add and subtract from the top of his head. Before I knew it, he was doing multiplication in his head. He was just that good with numbers.

Some kids are naturally drawn to certain subjects. Some kids are good at reading; some kids are good at math. He loved numbers. He loved math, and that came naturally to him. I'm so glad I put him in a private school in the beginning because I truly felt that they required higher standards from the students. It was a great foundation for my son.

PJ WITH HIS VIOLIN

I only took him out because that stuff was hurting my pockets. Private school was no joke. That $900 bill came in every month. I took him out of private school when he graduated pre-k4, and then he got accepted into the school he was in when he passed.

He was at home with my mother until he was three years old. My mother is amazing, and I appreciate her for all of her sacrifices, but I didn't expect my mother to be a school teacher.

PJ AND HIS GRANDMOTHER

I put my son in a Christian private school so he could get acclimated to how school worked and also get a foundation for his education. I didn't want to wait until he was 5 to go to school and not have that experience. I felt he would have been behind. So, I sacrificed that year and put him in private school when he was 4.

PJ and My Relationship

So, I'm a structured parent. Certain things I simply ain't letting slide. Certain stuff you just can't allow from kids. They are kids and they don't always know right from wrong. I don't judge other people for how they raise their children, but I do not tolerate disrespect. Not only being respectful to adults but also being respectful to yourself and your mother. I'm saying there are certain things you just can't do or say.

Once you allow a child to do something you don't approve of, you can count on them to continuously do it. Then, as they get older, you best believe things will get worse. So, respect was one of the main things I was heavy on with him. He respected me when he went out and stayed at other people's houses. Many people thought he was the greatest kid because of how respectful he was. If I asked him to do something, he did it. I'm saying with no hesitation he might back talk a little bit, but it ain't disrespectful back talk. He was still going to get it done.

So, I will say, for me, my overall relationship with PJ was akin to a best friend. He was somebody I knew would never turn his back on me.

PJ LOOKING DAPPER

He wiped tears from my eyes at night when I was crying, going through my divorce. He went through all of those emotions with me, and then he saw the overall outcome of what sacrifice looked like and what turning pain into purpose looked like as well. He helped me get out of that dark space and showed me that I still have to work hard and push hard for him, and that's what I did. I feel like the greatest day of my life was the day I was able to give him our house. He was my best friend; he was my accountability partner. PJ was the person that I felt loved me the most on earth. No one could ever love me more than my son. He looked up to me in ways that I didn't see myself worthy enough to be a role model for. He helped make me who I am today because he was a kid who understood what sacrifice looked like since I showed him that. He was a very appreciative kid, never ungrateful.

Space for PJ to Be His True Self

I always desired to hold space for my son to be his true self. I guess I learned from being a lesbian how important it was for me to be my authentic self. My mother never talked me out of being myself, so how could I do that to my kid? I couldn't ever shoot down any of his dreams or whatever he desired or wanted. I was raised by a mother who let me be myself. She made it easy for me to come out at an early age. I was in the 9th grade when I came out to my mother. She gave me the space that allowed me to be free, so I felt it was only appropriate that I afforded my son that same opportunity. I would just be the overall decision maker when it came to his wellbeing. I would let him give his opinion, but overall, I made the final call. For the most part though, the decisions that he made for himself were good ones. This is something that I think some parents have a hard time with —creating space for a child to be themselves but also having boundaries.

I created a space where he could express himself. I would explain to him if it was a bad decision or something, or if I felt like he was going in the wrong direction because he was allowing his fears to interfere with his thoughts and his decisions, I would step in and let him know. There was a point in time when PJ wanted to give up on football because he played with a team that was very competitive. When he got out there with kids who were the same size as him and played as hard as him, he had never experienced that before, and it made him want to give up. But I felt that he had to conquer this newfound fear. He had to believe in himself and know that he could still be the best PJ he could be. He had extremely talented people on the team and I reminded him that his team was powerful. I assured him that his fears couldn't overpower what God had for him. And that's really where his affirmations were born, from my son battling with his own fears because he didn't want to have to work hard at something he loved since he never knew what working that hard looked like. How could you be scared to work hard for something, and you were already doing it? You just were doing it better than the kids you were playing with before.

I explained to him, "Now that you're with more competitive kids that do the same thing as you and work out the same way you work out outside of practice, keep your head up. Hey, that just means you have to work ten times harder now. That's it. You can do it. You just have to believe in yourself."

I reassured him by working out with him and showing him that, look, man, mommy's out of shape, too. We worked out together in the yard and at the park. I reassured, validated and encouraged him consistently. Once he had that confidence, he was a beast all over again.

I can honestly say when he died, PJ was at his all-time best. He was about to be great. Like seriously, his confidence level was at an all-time high. And that came from just me building him up with affirmations and praying with him. I feel like a lot of people try to live through their kids because what they see for their kids is what they once wanted for themselves. But you gotta let your kids live their own lives. I believe my affirmations and prayer method made a huge difference. I explained things to PJ. I desired for him to be confident in every area of his life.

Even through the divorce, he didn't understand it. He was three. I still communicated with my son, sat him down, and explained that his parents weren't going to live together anymore. I explained where everyone was going to be living and consoled him when he cried for my ex-wife sometimes. I think for about 3-to-6 months, I dealt with bad behavior from my son just because he didn't fully understand. He was three. He was still a toddler. So, trying to explain something like that to him, that he'd been disconnected from somebody he was with all his life, was really hard for him to grasp.

Reassuring him and rebuilding his courage and hope backup was something I really had to focus on during that time of his life. I held space for those behaviors because those behaviors weren't normal. It wasn't him. It was because he was hurting from something. I would still discipline him if the behavior called for it. Though I would explain why I was disciplining him because he needed to know that at the end of the day, certain behaviors would not be tolerated. I wasn't going to tolerate him having fallouts and all of that every five-seconds. We weren't going to do that.

I told him, "You're going to sit here and read a book. You're going to sit here, not watch TV. You're going to sit here and understand what you're doing."

I explained the divorce to PJ. I explained my grandmother's passing to PJ. I explained sacrifices to PJ. I explained the home buying process to PJ. I feel that since I've always done my best to explain life and what was happening around him, it helped PJ connect the dots.

Parents literally have to connect the dots for their children because their minds don't work like adult minds. You have to literally do it for them. And before my son transitioned, he was able to see everything full circle. A lot of people don't get to see that, but my PJ was able to. We started here and then we ended up there. I was an example of what can happen when you sacrifice appropriately, the right way.

Conscious Parenting

Since I communicated with my son, he knew the sacrifices that affected him weren't because he was bad. He knew it wasn't because he didn't deserve certain things. He knew it was for a bigger purpose. But when people don't talk to children about what's happening around them, children can come to their own conclusions that can have nothing to do with what's happening. Too many adults haven't learned to effectively communicate with children or even with other adults. And if those adults have children, then their inability to properly communicate affects their children in a negative way. I worked on myself to become a better parent; I desired to be not only emotionally aware of myself but, more importantly, aware of where PJ was emotionally and mentally. I worked to be more of a conscious parent.

I was always a decent communicator. It was just hard for me to sometimes express myself because my mother was the type that didn't communicate with me in the same manner that I communicated with my son. So, everything that I knew I didn't have as a child, I tried to be ten times better as an adult with my child. That's how a lot of things really transpired for me when it came to PJ. I knew for a fact that some of my adult behaviors, especially regarding my romantic life, came from not getting certain things as a kid. So, I was conscious and alert with my son. I didn't want him to have these types of problems when he became an adult because that was going to be an issue that somebody else had to deal with. So let me, as a parent, give him what I didn't have. That was why I was so gung-ho about a lot of things when it came to PJ. I wasn't talking to him like an adult, but just being transparent with my son. I'm grateful I got the opportunity to pour into my son in that way. I truly appreciated the work involved with being his mother.

I feel like I prepared for my son. Some people just get pregnant and learn as they go along. Not me, though. I prepared for my son. I was excited for my son. I wanted my son. And that's how he was created. I feel like it's a little different path for me because mental and emotional preparation was already put in the works before PJ was born. I knew what I wanted to do for my son because I didn't have it all and I wanted him to be great.

I think more people should have an honest conversation with themselves about how much they actually appreciate the work that it takes to be a mother. Even if you didn't prepare before your child was born, you can still prepare for the next stages in your child's life. You don't gotta play it by ear indefinitely. At any moment, you can take the time to prepare yourself for what's coming up next so you can be ready for it. As much as you can, obviously, because kids can throw you a curveball.

PJ AND HIS PUPPY VALENTINO

When I think about being a mother and the title motherhood, I know for a fact that I did an amazing job with my son. I was that mother who would do anything for her child. Somehow, PJ helped me to unlock a version of me that I didn't even know existed before. I could always decide something in my head and make it happen. I kind of felt like I was forced to figure things out for PJ's sake, and I honestly didn't really know where to start, but I knew I had to do right by PJ. That burning desire to unconditionally love and provide for PJ unlocked a new version of me.

PJ was a Blessing

PJ is going to live as long as I breathe. I will carry on his legacy. In the midst of this tragedy, keeping his legacy alive has been a blessing. He was an amazing blessing. He's my biggest blessing. It was the best decision I could have ever made at the age of 25: having my son. My son taught me from day one honestly, what sacrifice looked like with every battle that we fought, every battle that we encountered, and every battle that we struggled with. I appreciate all the lessons I learned from him, even in this moment, because it made me who I am right now to be able to deal with the grief of losing my son. My son continuously blessed me and always made me feel complete. So, when I lost my son, a lot of people thought that I was going to lose myself, but I couldn't teach my son not to lose himself when he was living and contradict myself now that he's gone.

So, I had to vow not only to myself but to my son, that baby, I know you ain't here, you in a better place, but I'm going to stay consistent with doing what I'm supposed to do and the calling that God put on my life. God didn't take my son from me. The streets did. The devil did. God is just now transforming my mind and my body and my spirit and my soul to do the work that he already instilled in me. It was already instilled in me. So that's how I'm able to function, keep moving, keep pressing on because I always put in my son to never give up. Always believe in yourself because, without God, I ain't nothing, yet with God, I'm everything.

I just keep God at the forefront of my life. Honestly, I was just telling my friend yesterday; I said, "Man, just seeing me really trust God in my weakest moments and seeing him transpire in my life the way he has since my son passed... I can't let up on God because he just continuously bless me."

In spite of my hurt, despite my pain, God still got me. He's still holding on to me. He still got my hand, and He's still leading me in His footsteps, and I'm just following Him.

And like I tell everybody, my motto is, "I live to see my son again."

And I live by that and I will do whatever it takes to keep living by that. I know that my son is with God, so I have to do everything that God put forth for me. Whatever He put in front of me, I got to walk through them doors and just have faith. That's all it is. PJ was and still is everything to me. He was the biggest blessing I could ever ask for. When, or if, I have more kids, that's another blessing added to the blessing that God already gave me: PJ.

I try to do the work and continuously make my son happy and proud, and to let him know that, "Hey son, they tried their best to break me, but it ain't work."

I still push through. It's like the irony of raising my son, and the teachings I poured inside of him are now what keeps me going. Everything I told my son to try to instill in him is what I live by now. And that's not saying I wasn't living by it then; it's just saying that I'm really putting forth the effort to really believe in myself because I could have given up.

A lot of people just knew I was going to lose it. They knew that I breathed my son.

Like, everything was about my son. They knew my life for eight years was that of my son. To lose him and now live two years without him, I feel like I'm doing an awesome job. Yes, almost like this ministry that I'm in, I was already in it; it just wasn't public. It was real life. It was going on under my roof; that was it. How I move now was PJ's normal; it was how we moved. The only difference is that now I'm moving through life without him physically with me. How PJ and I lived our lives with our belief system is proof it works. It works, man.

When I was going through the process of getting my house, my hashtag for that whole time frame was "God's plan, God's plan." And I still live by that to this day. God's plan at the end of the day. When you just trust Him, even in the weakest hours, man, He's going to show you His work. You just have to believe and trust in Him and just have that faith. That's all it takes.

It doesn't take a lot of work. People just don't want to put in the work within themselves with the traumas that they face in life. You have to work on yourself, and you have to be willing to put in the work to know that God's got you. I am not going to worry about them bills cause they are going to get paid. God's going to make a way. I'm trusting Him. I am not worrying about it. I am not stressing about it. We allow stress to overpower our faith. I don't do that.

I feel like there's a miseducation of faith. Some people don't take any action in the direction they want to go, they pray about it, wake up in the morning, and still worry about it. That's not faith. As you pray and believe, it's done. You leave that worry on the table. You pray about it. You keep moving. You still go to work, or you're doing whatever you've got to do while knowing it's already done.

Proud Mom

I've done the homework. My job now is to just grant him the legacy he deserves. So, I always try my best to put forth the effort in order to get the job done. I'm just following my God-given assignment. That's it, that's all. And that's what's keeping me going. So, I'm gonna stick with it because it's working. I've been in a very positive space lately. My son is proud of me. So I don't feel any guilt. Like,

I'm all right. Because I know he's all right. So, at the end of the day, I got to try and get there. That's all I'm doing. I'm down here just doing what I have to do until my clock expires. You got to live well. I'm just trying my best to just do what I'm supposed to do. Keep pushing through whatever opportunities God throws at me.

MY SON AND I

CHAPTER THREE

His Last Play

When I put my son to bed on Thursday, August 19, 2021, I had no idea that would be the last night PJ would ever sleep in his bed again. PJ spent the weekend with his best friend and his family. When they brought him back home on Monday, August 23, 2021, PJ, my stepson whom I affectionately call "Baby Boy," and I were hungry, and we were figuring out what we wanted to eat. PJ wanted Taco Rock in Virginia, while Baby Boy wanted McDonalds. So, we went to McDonald's first because Baby Boy wouldn't eat tacos. Then we drove to Taco Rock and took his

McDonald's inside with us. I ordered tacos for PJ and myself before we all sat in there and ate. We were eating, you know, chilling, talking, having regular conversation, the normal situation for us. I got full after about one and a half of my tacos.

"PJ, you want the rest of my tacos?" I asked him.

He replied, "Yeah."

So, he ate the rest of my tacos. They were salmon tacos with real salmon with the sauce and stuff on it like coleslaw. Once we left Taco Rock, PJ had enough of us. He was ready to make another move; he never wanted to stay home.

PJ WITH HIS BEST FRIEND

"Mom, can I go back to my best friend's house?" he asked me.

"Um, let me call his mom."

So, I called his best friend's mom, and she was cool with him spending the night, so I dropped PJ off. Once I dropped him off, I didn't see him for the rest of the night. That was Monday. My youngest and I went home to chill. It was the Summertime, so people and kids were at my house; everybody always stopped by or stayed at my house. Later that night, I got a phone call from my oldest nephew.

"Our little cousin got into something," he said quickly.

I asked, "What do you mean he got into something?"

"He got into something deep, man. Like youngin' started shooting, and they had to shoot back. His man's got hit. I'm about to go get them a hotel," he said.

I said, "All right, man. Slim, you need to go home. You need to be safe."

"All right, I'ma call you when I get in the house."

He ended up texting me when he got home. He was safe. So, I texted my younger cousin.

"You good? I'ma come holler at you in the morning. Just let me know when you home. I'ma come holler at you in the morning. Me and my brother and my nephew, just to make sure you good."

He replied, "All right, cool. I'm good. I'm safe. I'm at the hotel."

Tuesday, August 24, 2021

I woke up the next day worried about my cousin because of the situation he had gotten into with his friends. I picked up my brother and my nephew and we ended up meeting him at my aunt's house. This is the location where my son would later be murdered. So, I go there that morning. My cousin came out of the apartment, real nonchalant as he approached me.

"I'm good. I'm all right. Y'all don't got to worry about nothing. That ain't my beef," he said assuredly. "That's my friend's beef. I just was there. So, I had to shoot back."

I said, "All right... cool. You sure these youngins don't know where you live at?"

He replied, "Naw, man. It ain't got nothing to do with me." He was sticking to the script.

I said, "You sure, man, before we leave? Like, cause for real, like this ain't cool. Your mother in here, your brothers in here. This ain't cool."

He said, "Naw, these niggas some suckers."

So, I went about my day. I ended up dropping my brother off and going back in the house. I was back working online at my job all day. I called PJ later in the day.

"Are you going to football practice today?" I asked him. "Ya'll got a scrimmage against Rosedale. Are you going to play in the scrimmage or are you going with Marquis to his doctor's appointment?"

He replied, "Naw, mom, I'm going to play."

So, PJ's best friend's mom dropped him off at my aunt's house around 5:15 pm. I was already waiting for him. I get PJ then we leave and head to the scrimmage. This is the first scrimmage of the season, so I'm giving him my normal pep talk, helping him to get in the right headspace. We met with his team at their practice field, which was close to the

Commander's FedEx field at the time. The team said they were going to walk over to Thomas Pullen, where the game will be.

So, I asked PJ, "You gonna walk or you want me to drive you?"

He said, "No, ma, I'm going to walk with my team."

They had to walk through the woods or whatever, but he walked with his team. So, I drove around there. It wasn't too far, probably a couple blocks away.

When I made eye contact with him, I yelled, "You good?"

He was like, "Yeah, mom, I'm good."

I said, "All right, man, ball out. I love you!"

And he balled out. My son was crushing shit. The other kids were too small. They couldn't do anything with him. They were triple-teaming my son. They had three kids on my son at one point in the game. PJ was still dogging them and pancaking them youngins. He was smashing them into the ground and getting to the quarterback. He had like two sacks. He had like five pancakes. He was doing it. He was crushing it, dominating. The other team ended up quitting.

When they quit my son, he came over to me and said, "Ma, I was dogging them. These youngins too small for me. I had five pancakes, Mom. I was crushing it!"

He was talking his shit and I let him. When it came to football, I let him be himself. I dapped him up and said, "Good game! I'm proud of you. You did a good job."

Parents from the other team, from Rosedale, came up to my car, complimenting my son.

One parent said to me, "That was your son?"

I said proudly, "Yeah, that was my son. He is in the back seat. You can't really see him because of the tints." So, I roll down the window.

The parent said to my son, "You like that, Slim. You good," as he was dapping him up. The parent continued, "Man, you like that. You good for real. Like you like that slim. You got to keep balling."

That was truly a proud mom moment for me. Everybody was coming up to him, complimenting him and hyping him up. Now I was ready to go because, mind you, it was Tuesday. This is Taco Tuesday. We always cook tacos. My partner showed up to show her support for PJ. I called her to give her the update.

"The game ended early, so there's no point for you to walk down to the field. I'm going to run past my aunt's house, then go home."

Man, I was hungry and tired. I really didn't want to do anything. Those were my emotions at that moment.

She responded, "We can chill over there for a little bit."

Then PJ said, "Yeah, Mom. I want to chill with my cousins."

I get it. It's his favorite cousins. He wants to chill with them. He wants to eat his food and play the game a little bit.

So, I said, "All right, cool."

Boom. So, we ended up going over there to my aunt's house. My aunt lived close to Thomas Pullen. It's literally a light away from my aunt's house. So, you go through the light on Brightseat Road, and my aunt's apartment is on the right. The first apartment once you go through the light. So, my girl met me there. She was already there when we pulled up. I backed into a parking space.

PJ WITH HIS FAMILY

It was like my aunt's apartment, my girl's car, and then across the street, it was my car. So, it was like the street was in between us, the apartment, and my girl's car. My son was talking trash the whole ride home. My son hopped out of the car when we got there and ran to my girlfriend's car, which was in front of my aunt's patio. That's how we walked into my aunt's house, through the patio. PJ was telling my girl all about how amazing he did at the game. He was proud of himself. In the midst of that moment, he was so proud of himself. He conquered something because my son really was going through a lot that whole summer, just denying himself, feeling like he couldn't get better. And that game really boosted his morale. Now, it seemed like he had upgraded his mindset. He was so excited. My two nephews and my cousin were sitting on the patio.

So, after PJ told my girl all about his game, he said, "I'm a little hungry," to her.

She replied, "Yeah, I got your food."

So, I grabbed his food, and PJ started walking towards the apartment where my nephews and my cousin were. Then you know he had to tell them all about his game. They were dapping PJ up and gassing him up. I go into the apartment, and PJ followed behind me. I took his food in the house. I sat it on the table right at the door. My aunt's table was right there at the door. I sat his food right there.

I said, "Nah, take your shirt off. Take off the sweaty stuff."

And I made him wash his hands in the kitchen. After that, I kind of like washed his neck a little bit and washed his face a little bit because he was so sweaty.

Then I said, "All right, man, sit in here, eat your food, but we ain't gonna be here long cause I'm tired for real. Like play one game and we done."

When he sat down at the table, he took a bite of his taco. It was a salmon taco.

He said, "Ma, this joint bussing."

So, my girl didn't just bring him tacos; she brought some for me and her, too.

I said, "It's like that?"

He said, "Like no, for real ma, this joint bussing."

I didn't know it at the time… but that was my son's last words to me. I walked out the patio door, which was right there where PJ was sitting. It was like the patio door and then PJ's seat. So I went around PJ, went out the patio door, and I went outside. I was telling everyone what PJ had said about the tacos. Then I sat in my lawn chair, which probably was about like five or six feet away from my son. He was inside the glass patio door. I was outside the glass patio door. I was the furthest away from him. Everybody else was kind of closer to him. I opened up my taco in the foil. My girl was sitting next to me, my big cousin, my nephews, and my younger cousin, the cousin whom I had gone to talk to that morning. He was the closest to the street.

I sat in my chair and said, "Yeah, PJ sicing these tacos. Let me try," so I bit it then said, "Naw, he ain't sicing these tacos. They are good as shit."

My girl grabbed my taco and bit it.

As soon as she bit the taco, I said, "That joint good?"

And I think the last words she said to me was, "Yeah, this joint good."

Then they started shooting. My first thought in my mind wasn't they shooting at me. It never dawned on me that they were shooting at my cousin. It dawned on me just to protect my lady because she was the closest person to me. So, I grabbed her out of the chair cause she ain't even realized they were shooting. I yanked her out of the chair. As I was ducking down to the ground, I yanked her to the ground and yanked her toward me.

She yelled, "What the fuck? They are shooting?"

I can see the fire coming towards us. So, I know they're shooting at us. I was never thinking that my son was going to get shot because he was in the house. PJ is all right. I never thought that shit.

I'm yelling, "Get the fuck down! Get the fuck down!"

It probably was maybe 15 to 20 shots. It's two people shooting at us. So, in my mind, I'm already calculating stuff cause I'm just like, look, 9 millimeters only going to hold about 10 bullets. I'm calculating everything in my head for real, but I just want to protect you know, I'm saying that's my first thing to protect. So once the shots stopped and the glass shattered on the patio from the sliding door. That's when everybody hopped up and ran into the house. I ain't run in the house; I stayed outside. I laid on the ground because I was still stunned. But all I could hear in the midst of gathering my own thoughts was someone yell, "PJ get the fuck up! Oh my God, PJ! What the fuck! PJ, get the fuck up!"

All I hear is all of this screaming. It's like seven people screaming his name. PJ wasn't in the house by himself, though. He was in the house with his God-brother. But his God brother went to the bathroom when the shooting happened. My son was at the table by himself. So, when his God-brother came out of the bathroom, that was the first thing he saw, everybody screaming and crying. I'm the last one to get up once I heard PJ. I just got up.

I said, "I know y'all not saying my son got shot."

I got up real fast off of the concrete and there's glass everywhere. There's blood everywhere. I go through the sliding glass door and my son's head is on the table. My son got shot in the head. My son got blood everywhere on the table. He laid on top of the game controller that he was playing Play-Station on with his God-brother and his taco that he was eating. He was laid on top of that shit. So, he got shot in the head and he got shot in the leg. The first thing is, I'm not thinking about him getting shot in the head, I'm thinking, *Well, maybe my son just got shot and he gonna be alright.* I don't know where the strength came from, but I picked my son up. I picked my son up, not needing help from anybody else. I picked my son up like a baby and I took him to the ground.

I cried, "PJ, get up, young. I need you." I'm just telling him all this in his ear. "Like, slim, like, I need you slim." None of this shit can take my baby away from me. That's my baby. I cried, "Bro, I need you, bro. Like, I love you to death, slim. Like, you all I got."

My son wasn't saying anything. He wasn't responsive. His eyes were closed already. He wasn't rolling or anything. His eyes were closed. My girl ended up coming over there and helping me. Holding him and shit like that. I tried breathing into his mouth. Do all that. I mean, I still got some techniques in my head, but at the end of the day, this is my baby. So, I'm not even thinking about it. But I tried my best to do what I could, tried to put air in his mouth while everybody was just screaming. My nephews, they're kirking out.

Trying to figure out who did it. I understood the anger.

But I said, "Y'all need to call 911.

Three to four people are calling 911 now. It was the longest 10-20 minutes of my life. Waiting for the ambulance to get there. When they finally got there, they took him out of my arms. I leave the apartment and I'm just maxing out because I'm just like, how could they do this to my son? He ain't deserve that. My son doesn't have anything to do with my younger cousin's nonsense. PJ don't got nothing to do with none of that. Like, how could you shoot my baby? This my whole baby; he doesn't deserve this.

When the ambulance pulled off, they had no flashes or lights on. I knew my son was gone. My girl had called my mother and my mother pulled up.

I said, "Y'all no funny my son is gone. They ain't got no lights on the ambulance. If it was an emergency to get him to the hospital, they would have on lights, and they don't have no lights on for my son.

At the Hospital

No one needed to tell me. I knew that my son was already gone. My mother and my brother, Sean, arrived at the scene, and they ended up driving me and my partner to the hospital. We had to still talk to the police for a little bit. So, we didn't just rush to the hospital. The ambulance had already left from Landover, Maryland, where we were, and was going to Children's Hospital in North West, Washington DC, with no lights on.

The hospital was about 15 to 20 minutes from the apartment. So, my mother's driving. I'm just praying, you know, just talking to God in my own way. Calling my family, telling my mother to run the lights. I don't care about none of that. I'll deal with that stuff later. When we finally arrived at the hospital, we parked in the emergency room area. And when we parked right there, they opened up the doors, and it was right at the entry where my son was.

The doctor met me close to the door as I was going to where PJ would have been in the hospital.

"Are you PJ's mother," he asked sadly.

"Yeah," I replied somberly.

He continued, "I tried everything I could do. I did everything I could for PJ…But he was already gone."

I didn't max out at that moment. My partner passed out. My mother was crying hysterically. Then it was me standing there. And I paid them no attention because, at the end of the day, it's like this is a moment for me, you know what I'm saying? And I walked over to where they let me in to see my son. He was lying on a metal table.

I was able to see my son, but all I could do was just stand there. I just looked at my son and thought to myself, *Baby, you didn't deserve this*. Like I wasn't hysterically emotional. I cried, but it was cries of anger because I was more mad than sad. My son didn't deserve any of this, none of it. He didn't deserve to feel none of that. He was a good kid. I'm just talking to him, just rubbing him, smelling him, kissing him. I knew he was not physically there. But I felt like he could hear me. I told him I love you. *I wish I could have protected you*, I thought.

That was the big thing for me. I felt like I failed him because I couldn't protect him in that moment. And just seeing my son, laying there with no clothes on, he just had his football shorts on. I was just looking at him, just paying attention to his body. I didn't even notice his wounds because they had been covered up. My son was shot at the side of his temple right behind his ear. So that was covered up. And then my son was also shot in his leg. A bullet hit him in his leg while he was sitting at the table as well. I was just talking to him and just looking at him so apologetically. I cried as I wished I would have gone home and not stayed at my aunt's house. I stayed back there with my son for maybe 30 minutes.

I never thought in my life of seeing my son lying on a flat metal bed. On a fucking metal flat bed. It ain't have no cushion or nothing. He was on a metal flat bed, like a metal table. It crushed me to see my son on a metal, flat, cold table. That shit was the worst pain ever that I could feel. I could never put anything on top of that. To see my baby, my 8-year-old son, lying on that table when he was just talking to me.

The last words he said to me were, "This taco is bussing."

That's the only words of his I could hear in my head. And to see my son lying on this metal bed, not breathing. He was cold as ice. That's a pain I could never imagine surviving. My mother almost passed out. My girlfriend fell out on the floor. Everybody had all these emotions and I couldn't be mad at them. I was just angry that I was even in that moment. I felt like I had to be a comforter to everybody and make them feel like we were going to be all right.

I said softly continuously, "PJ is in a better place."

My older son, he was so angry. I had to let him have his moment, though. He was throwing chairs, throwing tables and shit. He was tripping, you know, but he was so angry because it's just like, why not me? Why my brother? Like if anybody had a brighter future, it was him, you know? So, my oldest son was just having his moment. And I told them to let him have it. Let him mess up their stuff.

I don't care. He's fine. Let him have his moment. That was his baby brother he prayed for all his life. He was angry and I understood that. I had to tell PJ's other mom that our son was gone and never coming back. That was hard, but I just wanted to be strong for everybody in that moment. Life just really turned in an hour. We were all happy and laughing, not even an hour ago. My son was having his proudest moments in life. My whole life just changed in a whole hour. I can never take that back. I can never take that moment back. To feel that pain and anger and just like so many emotions going through me, but God was going through me for real because it's like everybody feeling how they feel, but his own mother that gave birth to him...still wants to save the world.

After I spent my final moment with my son, I walked out into the waiting room area of the hospital, and all my family and PJ's coaches were in the hospital. I don't know how they got the call that fast, but they got there. There were a lot of people at the hospital. And to be honest, my partner only made three phone calls. And for that magnitude of people to find out that fast, I don't even know. So, I know that she called his football coach. They all were at the hospital when I came out of the room with PJ. I'm just crying with everybody. Tears ran down my face as I hugged everybody. I didn't know how to feel. I was so numb.

My brother had prayed over us, so we all were prayed over. Before I left the hospital, I ended up going in the back and I talked to the chief of police for PG County. His name is Chief Aziz. He's my guy. He cried with me. He was just so, like, honored to know how spiritual I was. He reassured me that his team of officers would do whatever they had to do to find the guys who killed my son. On the way home, I just cried, probably the whole way home, just trying to understand it. Angry a little bit, but God just took over me again.

At My Mother's House

When I left the hospital, I went to my mother's house. The detectives probably called me about 20 minutes after I got there. But before I could get to my mother's front door, there were about 100 people outside of her house. Cars up and down the road. Like everybody standing outside. I don't know who called who. I don't know how it happened. But when I got to my mother's house, there were about 100 people there. Everybody just met me there. When I hopped out of the car, everybody ran up to me, trying to hug me.

I pulled myself together and said, "Man, y'all go home and y'all hug y'all kids. Cause guess what? My life just changed within the whole hour. Like my son was the happiest kid an hour ago. And my whole life changed in a whole hour. Y'all go home and hug y'all mother fucking kids. I don't know what else to tell y'all but to go home and hug y'all kids, man. Cause guess what? I ain't get to hug my son, but he knew I loved him. I told PJ that I loved him when he was on the field. That was the last time I told him, my son, I loved him…. was at the field. And the last time I told him I was proud of him was at his game. And the last words my son said to me were, "These tacos are bussing." Like y'all go home and y'all show y'all kids some love that y'all never have shown them before, like real talk."

PJ GIVING BACK TO THE COMMUNITY

PJ READY TO PLAY FOOTBALL

I went upstairs, and then the detectives called me.

"Your cousin isn't cooperating," the detective said.

"Send me a cop," I replied.

They sent me a cop, who came to pick me and my partner up, and we both went straight to the mother fucking precinct, and we pressed my cousin out.

At the Precinct with My Cousin

My partner was on it when she saw my cousin.

"Man, fuck you nigga! At the end of the day, you need to tell these people what they need to know. What's these niggas names? Cause guess what? You the reason PJ's gone!" she yelled.

He wasn't trying to say shit. We had to press him out. My son is gone because of his dumb ass and I couldn't say much. I had a long, exhausting roller coaster ass day. I appreciated my lady so much for speaking for me for the most part. She was speaking out of anger. But her anger was scaring my cousin because that's when he started talking; he started saying nigga's names.

"I just know niggas nicknames," he said. "I don't know their real name, but this their nicknames…"

She got him to talk. He just needed to give the detectives an inch, and they'd drive the mile. That was the craziest 24-hour period of my life.

Emotions All Over the Place

That shit was crazy. The more I talk about it, the easier it gets though. Do you know what I'm saying? But it's like, why is that? I shouldn't have had to go through this. I stayed at my mother's house for three months. My lady went to my house and got us some clothes because I couldn't go back to my house just yet. When I finally did go back, PJ's room was exactly how it was when he left it. My son wasn't a messy kid, so nothing was out of order. You might have had a dirty clothes basket, but that was it. But there weren't any clothes on the floor. The first time I came home, I laid in his bed to smell his scent on the pillow and cried.

It was hard, man. It was hard coming home. It didn't feel like the same home anymore. When I pulled up, I was emotional…

and now it's like my peace. But sometimes, I do feel myself never wanting to leave what I created for my son. This shit is hard sometimes because I really want to be my normal self, but my house is my peace. I worked so hard and sacrificed so much just to get this for my son, and he's not even here to enjoy it. That's the most painful part.

I think about the many days where he'd be like, "Ma, I want to do this, or Ma, I want to do that." And I'd be like, "Nah, man, we're trying to get that house."

I remember when I took my son to closing, showed him what sacrifice looked like, had the keys and gave them to my son, and told him, "It's yours."

And he ain't even here to enjoy it. Everything I sacrificed for my son taught me a lot. I don't think kids really understand the magnitude of the sacrifices that parents make. I'm saying I really sacrificed a lot. Many nights, I just let my son eat, and I didn't. And now my son ain't even here. I can honestly say that I know my son is proud of me. Not only do I just keep his name alive, but I'm doing everything I got to do to keep him proud of me. I have to try my best to do everything the right way so I can see him again.

I love my son so much, and I know that even though he transitioned, he still loves me, too. At least, that's what I believe. I'm happy to have found peace in my home. Everything I've ever done or sacrificed for my son was worth it. Nothing was in vain. Everything, down to the tacos my lady made, was worth it. I don't know how crossing over works when people die suddenly, but I imagine my son transitioned quickly and woke up on the other side with my grandmother and father welcoming him. I like to imagine him talking their heads off about how great he did at his game and how "them tacos was bussing."

My son had a glorious day up until that moment he was shot. My son ain't suffer. He died at the scene. They just couldn't tell me that until the doctor confirmed it. That's why the ambulance didn't have their lights on. The doctor had to confirm that he was deceased. So, my son died at 8:21 for real. And that's why we always take a shot. We always celebrate 8:21 because that was the time my son died. My son couldn't have been saved.

My son was shot in the side of his head behind his ear. So, my son was already gone from that one bullet, even though he got shot in the leg as well. And one thing I fought with myself in the midst of that, that healing, my son never knew what gunshots sounded like. He never encountered that because I never put him in situations where he encountered gun violence. I beat myself up for a long time because I thought, *Well, maybe if my son had heard the first couple of gunshots, he'd have dropped, or he'd have run to the back.* I fought with myself for a long time with that thought.

That was something I was really battling within myself. I never told nobody, I never said nothing, but I was just like, young, my son should have known what gunshots sound like so he could identify it when he heard it. He could have run down the hallway. I'd have preferred my son to get shot in the leg than in the head. I fought, and I battled myself with those emotions for a minute, always in silence.

I never told my son what gunshots sound like, but I'm a gun owner, legally. I'm a gun owner and my son didn't know what guns sound like when they went off. He only knew what the TV showed. He never heard it in person to be able to say, "Oh, yeah, them gunshots, let me run down the hallway, go into the bathroom, and protect myself." I never put my son in those situations where he had to encounter that, and it took his life. I beat myself up for a minute because I felt like I failed my son. I felt like a failure. I've taught him all the right things in life, yet I never taught my son how to survive. I've heard gunshots in my life, and while making sure he never needed to worry about hearing or worrying about that, I felt like I prevented him from saving himself that night.

After some time, I realized that I hadn't prepared him for how I was raised and where I grew up. I was preparing him for where he was and where he was going: A better life. That's it. I never wanted my son to encounter the bullshit and drama that I had to encounter in life. But it was still hard to know my son wasn't prepared when it's something that I knew could have saved him if I just taught him.

So, for a while, I was hurting. I was hurting myself mentally because I was so hard on myself for the slip-up; I should have taught him that shit. My aunt's house is a high crime area, but I never thought of it because I'm just like, all I did was take him to football practice, take him to his other grandmother's house, and his cousin's house. I thought these were safe places, and they weren't.

And now, when it comes to my stepson, I didn't even want him to go anywhere for a while. My lady ain't even want her son to go anywhere. We were traumatized. We wanted to feel like this was our safe place and we were going to stay here. We're going to stay in this house right here. We ain't going nowhere else.

It's such a harsh realization; you can't control any place, not even your own. You only can pray that people are trustworthy about the life their living. Now my trust is shattered. I literally talked to my cousin beforehand, earlier that morning. I did my due diligence, and I trusted him. I asked him. I wouldn't even have dropped his mother and his brothers back off because they were with me at the scrimmage. I wouldn't want anything to happen to them, either. Why didn't my cousin have that same love for his own mother and brothers? That's crazy.

My cousin knew what it was. He knew what he got into. He was dishonest. And guess what? Guess who is still there for him? His mother. He could have gotten his own mother's life snatched. His brother's lives could be gone too! He was so fucking selfish. He just thought about himself and his survival, and that's fucked up. Now my son is gone cause of that shit.

I just don't understand, man. It's crazy how some young people are now so self-centered. And their mothers and fathers bend over backward for them, only for them to just give everybody else their ass to kiss like we owe them something. Some parents don't want to accept that their child is a fuck up. I think some parents take it as a personal attack on themselves. They internalize their child's bad behavior and don't properly address it. So, I do believe it's a trauma thing. It's a self-reflection thing. It's like people don't want to take the time to reflect on what they created.

I still communicate with and am cool with my cousin's mother, but sometimes I look at the shit like, yo, if you would have just listened. When my mother was getting on her about a lot of shit, raising her kids, she should have listened. She didn't. And this is what happens when people don't listen. Situations like this—a harmless, innocent kid getting killed because of something someone else created. And this is also why people cut their families off. I don't have an issue with her, but she tolerated known, problematic behavior from her son. Behavior that ultimately resulted in the death of my son. In this instance, he was the company she kept.

Now, I'm super big on boundaries. People always say, "Family over everything." But now, I say, "Energy over everything." I'm an energy-over-everything person now. When it comes to his mother, I love my cousin's mother to death. I just pick and choose when I deal with people now. If I don't feel like dealing with you in a moment, I don't. But outside of that, sometimes it's just best for me to stay to myself and deal with you when I see you. There's never no love lost.

I even love her son, my younger cousin. But sometimes, I just don't want to hear the excuses. I don't want to hear the bullshit because you had a choice, and you are a part of the consequences. And sometimes people don't want to feel the full extent of the consequences. But this is what it is. And I can love you while not giving you access to me.

Then God Sent Me a Message

After my son was murdered, my cousin didn't get locked up right away. He got locked up months later. He went to my son's funeral, and he was around the rest of my family. My mother didn't even want him in her house, which was well within her right. My whole family was angry. They ain't want to fuck with him.

I said, "But that's not what God told me, though."

You stand in front of your enemies, in front of the people who disappointed you. I was the spiritual guidance for my family for months. I had to tell my family what God was speaking to me. Like, he made a mistake. We all make mistakes. He made a big mistake. But I still wanted him to know that he still had a family that loved him because that's what God told me. I had to listen to God over everybody. Even in my worst moments. God was speaking to me and telling me what I needed to hear in the midst of my pain, my hurt and my sorrows. When I was thinking about giving up on life, I had to listen to God.

And God really told me like, "You still need to be there for him. You still let him know he has a family who cares because that's what's going to eat him up."

And it still does. Because I still show love. I still take his calls sometimes or if his mother needs my advice. He hurt me to the core of my soul. Nothing and nobody can inflict pain on me worse than that of losing my son. But I still want to be there for the people that hurt me. You stand in front of the people that hurt you. You stand in front of them, and you let them know that God is still a loving God in spite of... and I let God use me in a way that I never thought he would use me. Overall, my love is all for my son. I birthed that boy. I heard his first cry. I gave him his first and last kiss. If I want to see him again, forever, I have to continue to live in my purpose. For that reason, I've forgiven the people who killed my son. I just had to forgive them all.

Public Forgiveness

The day my son was murdered, my lady and I went to the police station to encourage my cousin to talk. Afterward, we sat out front of my mother's house and just chilled. We stayed outside till about 12 o'clock the next day, the 25th. I never took a shower or brushed my teeth. And I got on the news probably around 10 that morning. The news had gotten in contact with my brother.

My brother asked me, "Do you want to do an interview?"

I said, "Why not? Because guess what? I want the world to know this is me. This is PJ's mother."

And the news crew came to my mother's house. I did an interview with at least three channels that same moment on the corner of my mother's street.

One interviewer asked, "What do you want to tell the people that killed your son?"

I said, "I forgive them."

My son died on the 24th. I forgave those people on the news live on the 25th.

I said, "I forgive y'all. Just turn yourself in."

That's the God in me, bro. That's the God in me. Ain't nothing else. So remember the number 21. That was my son's jersey number. My son died at 8:21, and they ended up catching the guys 21 days later after my son got killed. I'm big on numbers now, just like how PJ was in math. Nobody could understand what I did, but it's not for the world to understand. I'm serving God, not the world. Forgiveness is hard, but again, "I live to see PJ again." I have to live in purpose, and I can't have the mindset of the world to complete that mission. Forgive my people, forgive!

Cowards with Guns

I don't understand. Y'all could have walked up on my cousin and shot him. What's the problem? Y'all were right there, but why y'all ain't walk up on him and shoot him? Y'all walked up to my aunt house. My cousin was outside. He's the closest to the street. Remember, my girl parked in front of the patio. Then it's the street and then my car. My girl's car took at least 10 bullets. They were behind my car across the street. One nigga, stood behind my car. The other stood behind my partner's car and was shooting at my cousin, and missed!

My cousin ain't get no bullets. Both of my nephews got grazed by bullets. So they could have walked up on him, done it, and ran off. My cousin was literally 15 feet away from the niggas that shot my son. How the fuck you don't hit your target? That's crazy to me. They're cowards, and now everyone knows… and so do the people in prison.

As the year went on, I thought I would talk to the killer of my son. On May 13, 2023, my cousin Le Le was having a birthday dinner, and my older brother called from prison. He is in an Upper Marlboro prison, so no one probably put the stories together. Lo and behold, he's locked up with one of the killers. My brother was running praise and worship. Someone later informed him that one of the brothers was in his praise and worship group. He said he approached him and let him know he wanted one thing from him: tell my sister you're sorry. At the birthday dinner, I spoke with the young man. Something I never thought my heart could do, but I did it. Again, forgiveness isn't for him; it's for me!

"Hello, this is Tiffani PJ's mother."

"Hello, Ms. Tiffani. Just want you to know that bullet wasn't for PJ," the young man stated.

"While I appreciate your honesty, you owe me! You owe, you owe me my son. You need to return some love back into my community. I forgive, like I said before, but you'll hear it now. You need to help these young men. You need to save some young men by telling your story. That one-second decision changed your life forever. My baby didn't deserve it, but he's in a better place. I love you because that's the God in me, so return the love and help me out. I pray to meet you one day, so you know this isn't fake love. God bless you!" I ended the call and hung up the phone.

My whole thing is I'm big on restorative justice. But outside of restorative justice, I want to also make sure these young men and young women understand what they do to these families. You crushed my whole life, son. My whole life was my son. No funnies. No disrespect to my family but all I cared about was my son. You took all that shit away from me. Now, do I want to have another kid? It's like I do, but then I think of how fucked up life treats you. Do I want to keep my bloodline going? I'm not a dummy. I know I birthed an angel. I birthed a star. I birthed a king.

I'd be nervous, but I still want to have another kid because I feel like I'm not leaving a legacy on this Earth other than my son's, but guess what? When I close my eyes, who's going to fight for my son's name to stay alive? I always felt very protective of my son, but I felt like I failed on that day. I just hope my son forgives me and knows I was just being his mommy that day. I wasn't planning on being a bodyguard that day.

CHAPTER FOUR

The Importance of Mental Health

Before I had my son, I understood the importance of working on healing myself. I do feel like I had the capacity for my son. I think some of what's going on in our community is not realizing how important it is for parents to actively work on their own inner healing. When shit happens, cause shit happens. You have more tools at your disposal if you've been actively working on your healing. It's non-negotiable. You must heal.

Healing is not a luxury. Healing is a necessity. Healing is not just for pain. Healing can be needed for something that was taught the wrong way. So, healing has different titles and different caps on it. And my perspective on healing, to be honest with you, even before I had my son, I knew that certain things that went on with me wasn't right. I was taught wrong. So, I'm thinking about what I can do and how I can move the correct way. And now I know that what I was doing wasn't the correct way because I kept failing.

I was misled or I wasn't taught at all, healing is a necessity because at the end of the day, I never want to push my stuff that I did wrong on other people. So hurt people, hurt people right? And how I progressed in life was working on healing. Healed people can help heal people. And I love the healed version of me because I'm able to pass on the positivity in a situation that can be so negative, and grant people hope and wisdom. I can grant that because even in my situation, I knew for a fact healing was the number one priority that I had to focus on because if I didn't heal the right way, I wouldn't be where I'm at today, post my son's death.

I could still be in that dark space. I could still be in that space where all I do is drink alcohol and smoke weed every day. But how was that serving my purpose? Being healed, you have so much more clarity with life. You can hear from God better. I just prefer this side of life than the hurt side of life. And I'm not sitting here saying that I'm by far perfect when it comes to my situation, but I feel like I'm fully healed. I'm in a space where I can honestly say I'm fully healed from my situation because now I definitely understand my purpose. I sat in those dark rooms, those dark spaces and doubted myself; *Why am I still here? What the fuck? Why am I here, God? Why isn't PJ here? Like, what am I here for?*

When I actually sat in those moments, I asked God questions, because He's the only one who's going to give me the answer. I started just being quiet. And when I got quiet, it was like, *Well, maybe you should stop drinking Tiffani. Maybe you should stop using weed as a coping mechanism. Maybe you should stop running from the change and doing the unnecessary to fill an un-fill-able void.*

Me spiraling out of control was a sign that I needed to sit still and just listen for God's voice. Oftentimes, when you have anxiety, you also might have little clarity. Lack of clarity can make you frustrated. Frustration can feel heavy and weigh you down. This is not a place where you want to be making life-altering decisions. Nor is this a place where you want to raise your children. You need to focus on your healing, especially as a parent. Sometimes you just have to sit in silence, man. Distractions are the devil on Earth, and guess what? Life will have distractions. So you're never going to not have a distraction in your healing process, because it's the devil. As soon as you get a foot closer to God, he notices and doesn't want you to grow in that healthy manner. So, as soon as you are close to your blessing, there's a distraction. Keep your eyes focused on God and have some type of willpower, even if it's a little inch of willpower.

At the end of the day, like, Tiffani, man, look, you got 17 years in the Federal Government. If I don't go back to work, I did all of that for what? Then I would question myself: *But what do I need a job for? My son gone. What am I living for? What do I need? I don't need shit. I could go live with my mother and be nothing. But why?*

I worked so hard to get here. I worked so hard to give my son the best life. And guess what? I did it. So why am I about to give up on myself? That don't even make sense. Like, yeah, my son not here, but guess what? My son is in glory. I'm trying to get to glory. Shoot, I'm trying to get to the place where I don't have stress any more. I'll be living with my son for eternity one day. What do I have to do to snap myself into that thinking?

Whatever it could be any act of acting out that you're doing to avoid healing. But avoidance with healing comes from fear. You can ask God the questions. Just talk it out. Because again, that's another myth in churches or in the Christian world that you can't question God. Don't you ask God. Don't you question God. He knows what you need. Then you're right. But guess what? If I don't ask him a question, how am I going to know?

So for me, I know what worked for me with God. Me talking to God like He's, my homie. Me sitting in the shower and just listening to gospel music and just praising God and then listening as He granted me all my answers.

Holding Space for Grieving Parents

There are certain times of the year where I am triggered and overcome with emotions. PJ's birthday, and holidays like Thanksgiving, Christmas, and PJ's Angelversary (PJ's death anniversary), those are triggering times for me and some of my family members as well. Those were the times when PJ was having fun with family and enjoying himself. PJ loved Thanksgiving. He loved Christmas too; that was his favorite holiday. For his birthday, we always did something big, a shebang. PJ's birthday is February 14, so my ex-wife and I never celebrated Valentine's Day; we made that PJ's day. And I still only celebrate my son's birthday. I still to this day don't celebrate Valentine's Day. When dating me, you either understand it or you don't. I remember when I was talking to a woman at one point, but she didn't understand my perspective. She wanted me to still celebrate Valentine's Day, either on the 13th or the 15th, but she didn't understand that I didn't want to do it at all. Not to speak ill of her, but I found it quite insensitive to even ask me to do that. If you can't accept the fact that I don't celebrate Valentine's Day because that's my son's birthday, you aren't the woman for me.

Being triggered by the holidays is hard because it's a point in the year where the major holidays are one after the other. And then it's like, I don't get a break until after PJ's birthday. That's why I'm intentional about my healing and desire a space to grieve and heal. I can't avoid holidays. I can't just take my feelings and sweep them under the rug. My body keeps the score. My body keeps track of when things happen during certain times of the year. So if I'm not really working on processing stuff through, I can just have more of an attitude and be viewed as a bitch. I don't have to have a calendar to know the exact date, my body will react. Then there's the building up of anxiety that I must be mindful of. Anxiety can build from anticipation of something that's inevitable that I can't control, which is Christmas. I can't control that.

People are going to say, Merry Christmas and Happy Holidays, and I can possibly get irritated by that but to be honest, I don't. And I might not feel like it's a merry one for me. I don't know if it's ever going to be a merry one for me. And sometimes I battle if it's fair to have a merry Christmas ever again. In this space now that I'm in, I give back to the less fortunate and that feels great.

I mean, I felt like even with my partner, the first year after PJ was murdered. I felt she wasn't understanding about me not wanting to celebrate Christmas. I understood that she had a child, but I don't think she understood that I didn't want to be a part of the holidays that year. It's like she tried to force that on me my first year experiencing the holidays without my son. And I was just so irritated. I just lost my whole kid. This is his favorite holiday. I'm not being selfish by far, but I really don't give a fuck about Christmas right now. You're not respecting that space that I'm in right now. Let me process what I'm going through. My son died in August. Christmas was in December. I didn't want to deal with that shit. As our kids got older, they wanted more expensive stuff. So I would be thinking about Christmas stuff in the summer. I would just be thinking about planning stuff ahead of time. And now all my thoughts and plans for my son, they no longer exist. That not only makes me sad, but I get emotional. Cause in general, my mind was always thinking about future stuff for my son. My mind is trained to consider my son and his desires. I would be done Christmas shopping by October. By the time the Christmas season came I would just be picking up little knick knacks. But his big stuff would have been bought by now.

And so like last year, I was kind of okay with it. Do you feel me? It was getting a little better. I just hate when people try to force their version of where I'm supposed to be at in my process. I don't like that. It's important to hold space for a parent grieving and healing. And we need people to hold space if we need them to hold space. You can't force healing and there's no time limit on grieving. People must grieve at their own pace. And some people can feel perfectly fine one moment and then, you know, go through it the next. And you are not in the position on the outside to tell someone how to heal and how to process their emotions. Sometimes you don't really need anyone to do anything per se, but just hold a safe space and that's it. Like, oh, you don't want to put up a tree? You know what, we don't have to do that.

I don't mind sitting down on the couch watching people open gifts. I'm not a jerk. But I don't want to be forced to participate in buying gifts, wrapping presents, putting up lights outside the house and shit. I don't want to do none of that shit. It's like, you know, people get offended, but how can you get offended when I'm the one living in the reality of this shit? I just feel like that is so insensitive, trying to force me to celebrate something that I'm not into no more.

My life has drastically changed to the point where I don't know what I want sometimes. I know I want to enjoy my life and whatever it looks like, I'm ready. My whole trajectory of life has changed. I just feel like some people are very insensitive to stuff and that just drives me crazy. Now I'm asking myself questions that I never had to ask myself before and that's a lot. Yeah, like now I want to travel the world. I be on that heavy now. In October, PJ's God-mother and I went to the Bahamas for peace of fucking mind. I wanted to go see blue water. I didn't want to be home at the time. It's just a simple fact that I'm in a different state of my life. This is not on purpose. It was not planned. It's not like I'm an empty nester. There's things that I'm able to do that I couldn't do before being a parent. I think sometimes when you have children, you're used to certain obligations. But then when you don't have children, you have lesser obligations. So now I go to work and come home, that's it but I enjoy working in the community.

Am I supposed to try to conform so that other people's reality doesn't have to be as different from what they use to be? No, my world is completely rocked. One would think people would try to make my world less different from what it was before because I took a significant loss. But that's something that also comes with appearance of strength, right? Cause nobody really knows what I'm thinking in my head. You may think I have it together, but no one knows how I feel day by day.

Romance and Grieving

After the death of my son, I became more intentional about every aspect of my life. I also became clearer on my purpose in life, how I want to live my life and the kind of people I want to share my life with. I used to be very quiet and content about a lot of things. I wasn't a pushover however I do think I was more of a "go with the flow" type of person. That all changed after I focused on healing, and I gain more clarity. I am very vocal now. I know everything I desire and that includes what I desire in a romantic partner. Also, I have higher standards from the onset of relationships. You either have it together or you don't. I no longer feel the need to provide a safe space for people to discover whether they have the capacity to be a great partner to me or not.

I've noticed that some interpret my direct-ness as disrespect, but it isn't. I get it, my clar-ity can be intimidating to someone who lacks clarity. However, I'm not going to make my vision fuzzy for you. I've been through arguably the worst thing that could happen to a mother. I know first-hand how short and un-expected life can be. I'm not wasting time on no one. With clarity I express myself well and either my partner can provide what's needed or not. Clarity affords less discussion. I'm not going to deal with certain things at this point in my life. I'm on a peace rally run right now. I'm enjoying life. I'm feeling good post tragedy. My life up to this point has helped me to solidify all my boundaries, standards, and requirements. I'm at a place of peace now. So, if you're not bringing that to the table for me, if you can't grant me understanding and respect, we can't do anything together.

I've worked so hard to get myself in this peaceful space since my son, I'm not letting nothing interfere with that. I don't care who you are, or how long we've been dealing with each other. I'm not saying everything must be perfect, no, life has ups and downs. But at the end of the day, the same work that I put in a relationship, is the same amount my partner should put in as well. So now moving forward, when dealing with romance and dating,

I also require them to allow space allocated for grieving because that's just a part of my life occasionally, especially around holidays and birthdays.

I do well most of the time. I spend most of the time in a very peaceful state. However, I've had moments when I'm triggered and would request a little tenderness from my partner. Dealing with grief and love can be a lot sometimes, however if you are with the person for you, I believe it's all worth it. It's an understanding. It's being attentive to the needs of a person. And if you have that bond and relationship, you should know this is a triggering time for her. I'm not going to take nothing serious. If you really care about somebody, you're going to understand the process and how it works because outside of my triggering times, I'm an awesome partner. And I'm not saying even in my triggering times that I'm a bitch to deal with, I could just be very emotional.

I'm a whole grown woman, I know how to control myself. So, for the most part, I'm not going to disrespect you if you don't disrespect me. I'm just at a different place in my life where peace is all I desire. I don't desire nothing else. So, if you can't offer a sense of peace, what are you here for? You're in the way. You're totally in the way.

I just want to enjoy my life, have fun, be at peace, and see my son again. If a romantic relationship aligns with the statement above great; if it doesn't, I don't want it. I once was at a point in my life where I wanted to marry again. I don't even think about marriage now. I know that my level of expectation for marriage is totally different from most people that live on this Earth. I don't even talk about marriage now because a lot of people don't take marriage as serious as I do. I want to be able to go into my marriage full throttle, giving my all and I would like the same energy reciprocated. I feel like in general in my life, the focus is myself and me being where I want to be here and how I want to feel.

After being so intentional about processing out stagnant emotions and actively working on healing, I realized the effort it takes to become authentic. It's work. I've noticed behaviors in some people that suggests there are areas in their life that requires healing, however those people don't find their behaviors to be problematic at all. Some people think that their normalcy is normal. No, it's not. You can recreate you, you can be whoever you want. They're like, oh, this is how I've been. You don't have to be that way. You can pick and choose aspects of you, you want to keep and aspects you want to change. People can explore and discover new ways of being. I think people think exploration is for, I guess, teenagers or 20 something year olds, but you can explore now with activities and think, just figure out what you like.

The first step is self-accountability, and some people don't see anything wrong with their perspective of thinking. So if you don't see nothing wrong with your perspective of thinking and seeing how your upbringing, your community life, etc has affected you; you are going to stay the same because you are a product of your environment. There are people who live amazing lives. Everything on Instagram isn't fake. I have friends who really travel every month.

If what I have as my boundary, or my standard, is not what you have for you. You gotta do what works for you. We're not the same. And it's not one is better than the other. You really want to be with somebody who thinks similar to you? Right?

It's just a no brainer, but you got to know what it is that you want from a person. I like peace. I want someone who can help to create and maintain peace in my life. Because I have a peaceful life already. I'm not asking somebody to clean up anything for me. Instead, I would appreciate someone who's looking for ways to create more peace. Wouldn't that be nice? That's what I desire. A person who naturally brings peace so I can maintain mine. That is a keeper, but first I had to know what I wanted.

I could have gotten lost in this tragedy. It could have been my son and I, like I could have gotten lost, not even just physically, I'm talking about psychologically, there's people who don't recover from this type of devastation. The last thing I want to do is to put myself in a situation where I'm having difficulty maintaining my emotions and all that other stuff.

While I've gained new boundaries and perspectives, I'm still very much blessed to have all the champions around me. Everybody, okay, the public, my family, my friends, and my football family. The football team says "Long Live PJ" every time we end practice, every time we end a game. Before a game is always "I believe in myself, I believe in myself. Without God, I'm nothing. With God I'm everything, Long Live PJ." Okay. Everybody still supports me even when it comes to his anniversary and his birthday. The love is always real. For one of his birthdays, I probably had like around 60 people in my house for Taco Tuesday. His anniversary, probably like a hundred people out there. I still get support and I am forever appreciative for all the love.

Gun Control & Mental Health

I am licensed to carry a gun in the state of Maryland. I'm not anti-gun, because at the end of the day, guns aren't meant to kill people. They're meant to protect. I believe a person that holds a gun should be a person that has the mental capacity to understand the use of a gun. I am anti-gun violence because gun violence is you using a weapon at your discretion and feeling like you can control and dictate who should be here and who shouldn't. I'm not a fan of that. I'm a fan of protecting my family. I'm a fan of protecting yourself and self-defense. I'm not just about to shoot my gun, just because you didn't let me get the last can of beans on the shelf at the grocery store. So, for me, I'm an advocate for conceal carry because I want to be able to protect my family and myself, but I also want to be able to protect the public, right? Because I can make those decisions because I have the mental capacity to understand self-defense and defending and protecting people in harm's way.

A big issue we have are people that hold these ghost guns. Ghost guns are illegal guns with no trace to it. Those ghost guns are the ones that are killing a lot of our children, a lot of our people. My son was killed by a ghost gun. So they haven't found the weapon that killed my son. But it was used in two shootings total. So it was used in the death of my son, and in a shooting that took place the day before my son. So that's a weapon that they probably will never find. It's been two years now. For me, I just feel like, you know, people should have the right to carry. But if we can get control of the ghost guns, I feel like the violence will go down.

It's not going to go down now, because we have government people who are into negative stuff. These gangs that are out here getting these guns from different states and stuff like that. We can't trace these guns. And the people that they're giving it to don't have the mental capacity to understand the real use of a gun. So that's how my son was killed. So you got two scary guys that really aren't about that life. They just shoot anyway, anywhere and hit people that have nothing to do with their beef. I feel like that's our number one problem right there, it is the mental health part. We were talking about it in my training yesterday. If everybody had a gun, right, every single person on Earth had a gun. And you must sign for the bullets, and it goes to your social security number. It wouldn't be gun violence because you'd be accountable for the bullet that hit somebody. Especially, if it was an innocent person that had nothing to do with your problem or self-defense issue.

So, it's all about accountability. You get back to this accountability word. But the government will never approve anything like that because they make so much money off the gun industry. They make a lot of money off death. They make a lot of money off of prison. So gun violence will never cease. We could just try our best to control it. There was a spike of gun violence in the US because of the pandemic, which caused a lot of mental health episodes.

The pandemic kind of opened up the mental health issues that was already there. So, you got hundreds and thousands of people with mental health issues with access to weapons. What do you think is going to happen? The gun spike is going to go up and it did. And it went up so bad that now it's uncontrollable. It's uncontrollable now.

I talked to the chief of police last week. A young girl got killed at a high school breaking up a fight. Her brother was down on the ground. Basketball star, good kid. Her brother got into it with some guys, and they tried to jump him. They pulled out a gun and shot her. She didn't have anything to do with it. She was just trying to save her brother and she got killed.

The thing I think about with guns is that guns aren't like weed. It's not something you can just grow in your backyard. If you left weed alone in the backyard, it could possibly just grow into the next yard depending on the conditions. It is just invasive. Guns require manufacturing, like at a factory. If you don't build it right, you can blow off your face. That's how intricate a gun is. You cannot make guns in your basement. Guns are not easy to make. So, a lot of the guns from Maryland right now, are coming from Virginia. So my whole kick to the whole gun control thing is holding states accountable. You know that these guns are coming from Virginia and states with open and carry laws and stuff like that. And then you have these manufacturers, these gun manufacturers in these certain states, right? They don't have top tier security and they get robbed, right? I believe if you get robbed too much, then you should be shut down. If you lose too much inventory then you should get shut down. Yes, I'm blaming the manufacturer for getting robbed because you should take extra security measures more serious and if you can't control your inventory you get shut down.

The gun industry is one of the biggest industries in the US, they don't talk about it. So that's why a lot of these laws get passed and a lot of things get swept under the rug when they come to guns and all they pay for the lobbyists. Because they want people on their side, you know what I'm saying, so a lot of stuff is never going to change. The only way we are going to end gun violence and get control of our community is getting mental help. The guns are never going to go anywhere, guns have been around since before the country was formed.

We just got to get our mentors in our community to teach our community about mental health. A lot of people don't understand the importance of mental health They really don't understand they may need mental assistance. And I think some people internalize mental health issues. A lot of this stuff has been passed down on to them. There's so many genetic predispositions that can put you in a certain place to make you more susceptible to certain things.

With that being said, you are still responsible for you. Your healing, is your job. I've communicated with a lot of guys who've committed murder, served their 25, 30 years, and they've all said the same thing. They wished somebody would have taught them certain things at a younger age, because the people that were exposing them to the bad things, didn't serve them well. They just wasted 25 years of their life and missed their children's entire childhood. You're a commodity and they want you to stay unhealed. It's a business, the system is set up for our culture to fail with traps that fuel the school to prison pipeline.

That's just one of the biggest things in our culture right now, becoming a product of your environment. Some people think that being a product of your environment is okay because it's normal to them. We just have to sit and take things to another level of severity. Some stuff we just know isn't right. Another thing is this public policy. So in our communities, we should cap out on liquor stores. We got one; we don't need another one for 10 or 20 miles; we can do that.

We can cap out on a lot of tobacco stores in one city. We don't need payday loan places. None of it serves us. In other neighborhoods they don't allow it. And it's not even that people don't allow it. You can't get a permit to open certain stores up. So this is why it feels like it's intentional. You do not accidentally maintain an environment. Environments are intentionally maintained whether you are consciously aware of it or not, you're maintaining it and it's on purpose. It should just be like no, we reached our max capacity.

My biggest thing is mental health. Being able to review what you're thinking, CBT, also known, as cognitive behavioral therapy. I feel like that's something we really lack in our community. We need new ways of thinking, people not knowing how to rewire their thinking is major. I took a class by a company named Roca. This program helped me a lot with not only how to handle the community but how to handle my thinking. The think, feel, do cycle is effective. CBT is a way of understanding the relationship between what we think, feel, do, and how that relationship impacts our lives. We're so programmed to the perspectives of what we were raised in. We don't see the bigger picture of how we could really be thinking in different aspects to get positive results. This encompasses a lot of things. There are different things that can happen, when you don't take care of your mental health.

I just want to heal us all. From everything, not just gun violence, but trauma as a whole. The trickle down effect is real in our culture concerning mental health. So when you understand how our brains operate, you know, from the top of our brain to the bottom of our brain, how those components of your brain really work. Often times we are operating in survival mode, which is the bottom of our brain. Given the conditions we don't even get the opportunity to use the top of the brain, which is the part of the brain that actually gives us those positive thoughts. As a result, many remain in survival mode trying to figure out how to survive daily. Why must we live this way? We shouldn't even be in survival mode anymore, but many have become a product of their community leaving them mentally stuck. So we have to learn how to change our way of thinking and want better for ourselves so we can get better for our children and grandchildren. Let's learn to break these generational patterns. We got to lift it. And that starts with the way you think, rewiring your thinking in order to see a broader picture of what life can offer.

Media, News & Cultural Image

Another thing that I would add with this discussion on mental health is that we need to validate people's experiences because it's true that as a culture we are constantly under attack. I am not going to gaslight somebody and their experiences. I'm fully aware we are under attack and it's not just community laziness. We are under constant attack. Media, music, laws and so on. So that's one of the things that I talk about when it comes to the news and the media.

I have a big story out in the Washington Post. I informed them that I'd rather y'all see the positive side of us than the negative side of us. I feel like y'all always pop up, the media always pops up when we cry, and y'all never make sure y'all follow up with us. The Washington Post followed me and five of my mother's for three months this summer, and they released a story on November 26, 2023. The story went on the front page of the national section of the newspaper. They didn't want it to just be a local story. They wanted this to go on the news and be a nationwide story because we just told them the severity of how we really feel. We feel like y'all are always there to catch us crying, but y'all never catch us when we're doing some positive things. All of my mothers are doing positive work in the community. And we're tired of just seeing mothers on TV crying because they lost their kids. But what about the mothers who lost their kids and are actually giving back to the community that took their kid? Not only did I tell the Washington Post that I told Channel 9, Channel 4, and Channel 5. I told them all, at the end of the day, call me when you want to hear something positive. Don't keep calling me when you want to hear some negative stuff. I'm tired of it. I want you to know that we are out here trying to work and be the best that we can be, despite our circumstances.

We could be somewhere losing our sanity, but we aren't. We are still giving back. We are still making sure that we are pressing forward and telling our kids stories and letting their names ring bells in the city. I always feel like the media always eats up the negativity and I'm over it. They call me back like you think you want to come in here for this or come in here for that? Sure, but don't call me for that negativity. Like I'm over it. When they call me about a killing, I tell them to connect with the parents. I am the co-founder of S.A.M, Strong Azz Mothers, L.L.C. Our organization helps all parents especially moms with the grief of their loss. All of our mothers have loss their children to gun violence. Our organization is focused on helping moms to heal now so they can aid in the healing of generations to come.

Generational Healing

Most times the media is capitalizing off the pain of our community. Which is why we need to be intentional about our healing and gain new perspectives about our community and upbringing. Those things can shed a lot of light and help us to better see ourselves so we become better people overall. Through my own self-reflection I realized how much I was actually like my father and how that played out in my life.

My father was a provider, so I thought just making sure that my family had everything that they needed financially was enough because that was how my father was. But my father wasn't there for me emotionally. My father was absent with the emotional provisions. My father was absent from just spending time with me. He just thought if he dropped off a check than he was doing his job. But again, that comes from generational lack of knowledge. I desired and needed more, and he didn't provide it. So, for me, my father was a financial provider, but he wasn't everything I needed as my dad. The emotional part, I kind of got that from my stepfather. Spending time with me, chilling with me, being at my games and looking in the audience and seeing my stepfather, but not seeing my dad.

But I do believe my father loved me. And then it got to the point where my father got sick. All I knew was to call my father when I wanted something. So that was a bad habit that I had until my father died. And I didn't have that anymore. I wanted more for my son because I didn't want him to ever feel those voids that I felt by my father by him not physically being there for me. I felt like he just wanted to be with my mom, but he didn't care enough for me. So when my mother got married, everything disconnected.

When I went through my divorce and I didn't know how to be the nurturing mom that PJ needed right away, I was mad at myself. I still be mad at myself sometimes, but that's all I knew then. So that goes back to that. You know better, you do better, right? And all I knew was what my father showed me. I'm supposed to provide for my family. And I'm supposed to go out here and work multiple jobs and make sure this money is here. Whatever you need for these kids, you make sure it's there. And then my divorce taught me something else. It showed a vulnerable side of me that I had to give to my son with no doubt because my ex-wife wasn't there no more. So that whole process showed me and taught me a lot about myself. My own traumas made me very vulnerable in my time of divorce.

I was in a vulnerable space where I understood this is what I desire, this is what I need. It taught me a lot. It really helped me. I really had to check myself and snap into the realization that at the end of the day, that baby came out of you. You got to grind for that child. You shouldn't have to beg no parent to do their job as a parent.

Where I Found Peace

Some people have to find that peace within themselves. I just look at my situation and I look at everything that God has carried me through and I'm like, well, I trusted God then I'd be a fool to not trust Him now.

He got me through all those times with a little bit of faith. And so just imagine when you have a lot of faith, and you just hand it over to him, you don't have any worries and no doubts, none of that. Guess what? It's been a great ride. I can honestly say 2023 has been an awesome year. God has granted me a lot this year just trusting his process, trusting Him and having faith over my life. Healing is a need and you gotta allow it to run its course. If you don't want it, it isn't going to work. I don't want to sit in here and be depressed. I don't want to sit in here and cry all day. I don't want to sit in here and be in a dark space all day. I don't want that. And you don't have to punish yourself. You can smile again. You can laugh again.

How to Take Accountability and Better Your Life

Being accountable is a profound commitment that involves accepting responsibility for our actions, fostering transparency, and being open to constructive criticism. It's a journey of acknowledging our choices and deeds, steering our intentions towards intentional goals, and tapping into our instinctive intuition for effective decision-making. This comprehensive approach to living is built on a foundation of accountability, specific objectives, and trust in our gut instincts to navigate life's twists and turns. Taking accountability is not just a task; it's a form of self-work, a commitment to holding oneself to a standard.

Reflecting on my journey, I graduated from the University of Maryland Eastern Shore in 2010 with a Bachelor of Science in Human Ecology. Often being questioned about its meaning, human ecology centers on the relationship between humans and their environment. Initially aspiring to work in education with young children, life took a different turn post-college, presenting opportunities with more funding than a teaching role.

Navigating the aftermath of losing my son, my background in psychology and lifestyle courses emerged as a vital source of support. In times of trauma, these fields became invaluable pillars, aiding me in coping and finding strength. This journey underscores the importance of accountability, intentionality, and trust in one's instincts for personal growth and thoughtful decision-making.

When I went to the Peace Academy of DC it proved to be a breath of fresh air, allowing me to delve deeper into my traumas and learn effective strategies for handling their side effects in my healing journey. The academy's courses were impactful for me, and I believe they can be equally beneficial for others. The initial focus on the three C's—acknowledging what we can't change (our identity) while recognizing the potential to alter our way of thinking—resonated with me. The broader connection of our communities in addressing gun violence, traumas, and the resulting negative behaviors was also a key aspect that caught my attention.

Understanding and addressing social disorganization necessitates a comprehensive approach, encapsulated by the Three C's: Conditions, Cognitions, and Choices. This framework provides a structured understanding of the factors influencing an individual's experiences and their responses to the surrounding environment. Through my own journey, I've seen the efficacy of this approach and believe it holds great potential for individuals grappling with similar challenges.

Conditions serve as the cards life deals us, encompassing elements like upbringing, environment, and household dynamics. These aspects, beyond our control, include understanding the impact of family dynamics at an individual level. Acknowledging influences like abuse, neglect, and the values instilled within the household is crucial. Considering neighborhood factors, such as violence and the state of community resources like community centers and recreational spaces, adds another layer of understanding. Recognizing these conditions is vital as they lay the foundation for an individual's experiences, shaping their journey in life. In simpler terms, conditions set the stage for the challenges and opportunities individuals face, and understanding them helps us grasp the complexities that influence how people navigate their world.

Cognitions delve into the realm of thinking and self-talk, offering a pathway to challenge and alter perspectives. Cognitive Behavioral Theory explores the interplay between thoughts, emotions, and behaviors, while restorative justice focuses on repairing harm and rebuilding relationships. Mindfulness cultivates awareness in the present moment, and Rational Emotive Behavior Therapy (REBT) addresses and manages irrational or unhealthy thoughts and emotions. Cognitions empower individuals to challenge thought processes, fostering a mindset conducive to positive change.

Choices effect your direction in life. Social disorganization can influence individuals to make unfavorable choices due to the pressure or strain imposed by their conditions. Recognizing the impact of irrational thinking, it is crucial to encourage responsible decision-making by addressing should statements, which involve identifying and challenging unrealistic expectations, as well as evaluating language used to express expectations (have, must, need statements). Additionally, examining patterns of avoiding accountability (excuses) and addressing limiting beliefs (I can't, I won't) can contribute to fostering rational thinking.

In essence, the Three C's framework underscores the realization that individuals cannot change the circumstances in which they were brought into this world. However, they do possess agency to acknowledge their conditions. By utilizing tools to address traumas, a foundation for healing is created, empowering individuals to make better choices in life. This comprehensive approach to social disorganization serves as a powerful tool in understanding and addressing the root causes of violence within communities.

Positive Parenting for Change

In delving into the discussion surrounding children's behavior, it's crucial to initiate an honest examination of parental behaviors. While acknowledging this truth might be challenging, it remains a fundamental step in understanding the complexities at play. Many parents are grappling with their own past traumas, and the repercussions are unfortunately seeping into the lives of their children. The impact is akin to stubborn stains that prove difficult to rinse away. To break this cycle, parents must address the root of their issues rather than opting for temporary fixes. Healing the wounds is paramount, setting the stage for lasting change.

Recognizing the impressionability of children at all ages, it becomes imperative for adults to set a standard through their actions. Children observe how we handle adversity, absorbing not only our teachings but also the influences of external entities. Engaging in continuous communication is key, as it lays the foundation for instilling values and morals. Parental prompts, akin to the simplicity of 1,2,3, align with the common needs shared by both parents and children. However, the urgency to nurture and teach basic life values often takes a backseat amidst the rush for children to grow up.

While it might be uncomfortable to confront, the reality is that many children reflect the behaviors they observe in their parents. The lack of active healing and intentionality in self-improvement from some parents significantly impacts their children. Addressing the behavior of children necessitates an intertwined conversation about parental roles, acknowledging that the two are intricately connected. To truly foster positive change in children, we must engage in an open and empathetic dialogue about the challenges parents face and the support they need in breaking detrimental cycles.

A Message to Children Whose Parents Lack Accountability

Dear Beautiful Soul,

I want you to know that you are not alone. In this vast world, there are people who care deeply about you. I may not be physically present with you, but my heart reaches out to yours with understanding, love, and empathy. I know that life has dealt you a set of circumstances that may seem overwhelming, but I want you to understand that you are not defined by your conditions.

Your journey began in a way that you couldn't control – your family, your upbringing, and the community around you. These aspects may feel like unchangeable parts of your identity, but there is immense power within you. You have the ability to reshape your thinking, to transcend the challenges of your environment, and to determine the trajectory of your own life.

Believe in the strength within your mind and heart. You can be a product of love, hope, and positivity, even if your surroundings suggest otherwise. While you may not be able to alter your past, you hold the power to shape your future. I, Tiffani Evans, a mother who cares, believe in you just as much as those who surround you with positivity.

I acknowledge that there may be moments of loneliness and despair, but I want you to see these moments as opportunities for self-discovery. Being alone doesn't have to be a negative experience; it can be a space where you find clarity and hear the whispers of your inner strength. When the world feels over-whelming, remember that within the silence lies the potential for positive transformation.

I understand the struggles, the tears, and the moments of hopelessness because I've been there too. But I found my purpose by taking moments of solitude to connect with myself and my beliefs. You have the power to do the same. Don't let the circumstances dic-tate your future. You are not bound by your condition; you have the ability to change it from within.

I want to be the voice that resonates with you, offering encouragement and support. Life may have thrown challenges your way, but there is still hope, peace, and a positive life waiting for you. You are resilient, strong, and capable of creating a future filled with love and joy.

With heartfelt love,

Tiffani Evans
How We Can All Help

Getting everyone involved. I want everyone to get help within themselves. How can we help the community if we don't fix the trauma within ourselves first? It will never work; we have so many damaged adults trying to help our traumatized children. The cycle will never end if oneself isn't healed first. I am pro-therapy. Therapy helped me before I lost PJ. Everything will come naturally.

"Let's Chat, No Cap" on October 10, 2023, was the eye opener I needed to understand the needs of our youth. The young people were nervous to express themselves in front of Prince George's County Executive Angela Alsobrooks and the State's Attorney, Aisha Braveboy.

Once we got on the topic of gun violence, I spoke, and the youth opened up. They expressed that their parents don't listen, don't ask, just have mood swings, and they sometimes feel unwanted. That was definitely hard to hear, but we needed honesty in everything. I asked them what we, as parents, can do to help better understand the youth, and they stated that parents need therapy. They have unresolved issues, and the youth feel like their parents don't know how to handle their own traumas.

This will now become a quarterly meeting with our youth. We want to stay on top of the issues to help decrease the problems in school and at home. The youth also stated that the pandemic played a huge part in their mental health. The two-year isolation from society left them depressed and misunderstood.

I want all readers to walk away knowing that through every trial, bump, and painful moment in life, there's still light at the end of the tunnel. Losing PJ wasn't the plan, and sometimes we lose sight of God's plan and think we are in charge. Keep God at the forefront of everything you do in life, and trust the process. We've all lived life on the bad side; just try the Father's side for once and see if you like that outcome. I want all the readers to get the help needed to heal themselves, so we can save our culture. The youth right now being our future is scary, but I still believe!

ABOUT THE AUTHOR

Tiffani Evans, the "Gracefully Spoken" advocate in the DMV area, draws strength from her faith to empower those affected by gun violence, notably parents who've lost children. Featured on national platforms like Inside Edition and local news, she tirelessly uses her voice to preserve her son's legacy and address the pressing issue of gun violence. Tiffani, a violence interrupter, believes in changing both external conditions and internal perspectives, endorsing Cognitive Behavioral Therapy for transformation. As the founder of the IamPJ Foundation and co-founder of S.A.M., Strong Azz Mother's, she actively supports youth affected by trauma and parents coping with loss. Tiffani is resolute in proving that her son's death won't be in vain, living each day with the mantra #LLPJ Long Live PJ.